MW00565096

R00111 13175

THE CINCINNATI REDS

PALM BEACH COUNTY PUBLIC
LIBRARY SYSTEM
3650 Summit Boulevard
West Palm Beach, FL 33406-4198

**MEMORIES AND
MEMORABILIA OF
THE BIG RED MACHINE**

Text by Bruce Chadwick
Photography by David M. Spindel

ABBEVILLE PRESS • PUBLISHERS
New York • London • Paris

Pages 2-3:
The 1919 Reds.
Frontispiece: A col-
lage testifies to just
what a powerhouse
the Big Red Machine
has been for decades.
Title page: Keeping
score in 1900.
This page: A jersey
and bat from the
winning sixties.
Table of Contents
(clockwise from
top): An aptly
named street out-
side Riverfront
Stadium; a bat from
the 1990 Series;
mementoes from
old Crosley Field; a
popular accessory in
1939 Cincinnati; the
prize in a 1910 ciga-
rette box; a lighter
from the 1950s;
early 20th-century
star Cy Seymour;
gas-station give-
aways from the
1950s; a "stand-up"
baseball card from
the 1940s; the local
hero showed up
everywhere.

To Margie and Rory.
—B.C.

For my special friend, Chuck Connors, who fully support-ed my art form and was a great player, truly dedicated to the game of baseball.
—D.M.S.

EDITORS: Stephen Brewer and
Constance Herndon
DESIGNER: Patricia Fabricant
PRODUCTION EDITOR: Owen Dugan
PRODUCTION SUPERVISOR: Matthew Pimm

Library of Congress Cataloging-in-Publication Data
Chadwick, Bruce
   The Cincinnati Reds : memories and memora-bilia of the Big Red Machine / text by Bruce Chadwick ; photography by David M. Spindel.
        p.   cm.
   Includes bibliographical references (p.) and index.
   ISBN 1-55859-514-7
   1. Cincinnati Reds (Baseball team)—History. 2. Cincinnati Reds (Baseball team)—Collectibles. I. Title.
GV875.C65C43 1994
796.357'64'0977178—dc20   93-37735
                                                          CIP

Compilation copyright © 1994 Abbeville Press. Text copyright © 1994 Bruce Chadwick. Photography copyright © 1994 David Spindel. All rights reserved under international copyright con-ventions. No part of this book may be reproduced or utilized in any form or by any means, electronic or mechanical, including photocopying, recording, or by any information storage or retrieval system, without permission in writing from the publisher. Inquiries should be addressed to Abbeville Press, 488 Madison Avenue, New York, N.Y. 10022. Printed and bound in Singapore.

First edition.

ACKNOWLEDGMENTS

We would like to thank all the collectors and fans who talked to us about their collections and memorabilia and let us photograph them at stores, homes, card shows, restaurants, and stadiums. We are particularly grateful to Willie DeLuca and his wife, Lynn, who let us spend an entire day with them, Cincinnati collector Bob Long, and transplanted Reds fan Steve Cummings, who let us fly to Seattle to photograph his gorgeous collection. Thanks also to collector Richard Miller, of Covington, Kentucky, and Joshua Evans, of Leland's, the New York sports auction house, for his assistance, and to the helpful researchers at the National Baseball Hall of Fame in Cooperstown, particularly its photo director, Patricia Kelly.

We'd also like to thank Reds public relations director Jon Braude and his staff and the athletes who talked to us, particularly Johnny Bench, Pete Rose, Gordy Coleman, and Barry Larkin.

Finally, our special thanks to editors Stephen Brewer, Amy Hughes, Owen Dugan, and Constance Herndon, and to Patricia Fabricant, our designer, who worked with us to make this another fine volume in the Major League Memories series.

BRUCE CHADWICK AND DAVID SPINDEL

CONTENTS

THE BIG RED MACHINE

There is something almost poetic about the nickname the Cincinnati Reds picked up in the 1970s, when they dominated baseball like few teams had since Abner Doubleday looked at his first fastball back in 1839. *Big Red Machine*—three words conveying size, power, precision, and most of all the steely edge of an inhuman and unstoppable engine. The great Reds teams of the late 1930s, the early 1940s, the 1950s, 1960s, and 1970s—even the 1990 world champions—were all winners, but since the spring of 1869, when Cincinnati fielded America's very first professional team, the Reds have never been an inhuman machine. If anything, the history of Cincinnati baseball is as marvelous as it is because of the very real flesh and blood characters, on and off the field, who have been connected to the Reds.

There was pioneering Harry Wright, the team's first player-manager, who took them on an undefeated national tour in 1869. The tour not only brought the Reds glory but helped sink the roots of what would become the national pastime in cities, towns, and villages throughout the country. There were the players on the 1919 team, who stunned baseball by winning the World Series against the favored White Sox, only to learn a year later that it had been fixed from the first pitch. There was the crack pennant-winning 1939 team, which in any other year would have

If anyone deserves to have his button in the middle of this contemporary collection of memorabilia, it's superstar Barry Larkin.

11

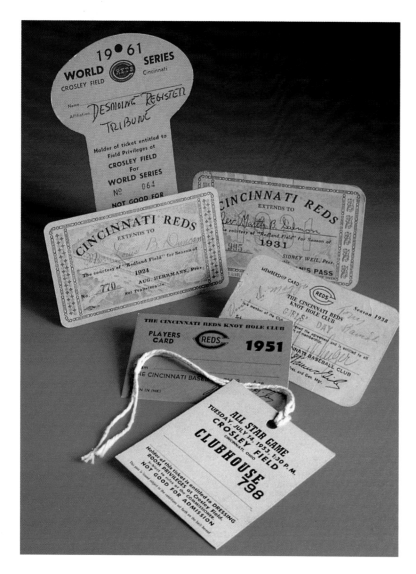

These press passes
cover seasons from
1931 to 1961.

won the World Series but had the misfortune to run into one of the greatest teams of all times, the 1939 Yankees. There was the 1940 team, which did win the World Series, with the help of a catcher who had to come out of retirement to help them do it. And what about big Ted Kluszewski, the heavy duty slugger whose arms were so big that the sleeves had to be cut off his uniforms to make them fit (resulting in attractive sleeveless uniforms for the team), or Wally Post and all of his home runs that seemed to fly over the exact same spot on the top of the left field wall, or Joe Nuxhall, who started his first major league game at the age of fifteen, or Frank Robinson, who was so good that the bumbling owners traded him, or Sparky Anderson, the gifted manager who took the Reds to four pennants and two world championships in just ten years?

What about the Big Red Machine of the 1970s: Johnny Bench, Joe Morgan, Tom Seaver, all Hall of Famers, plus superstar Pete Rose? Or later players, such as Barry Larkin, Tom Browning, Chris Sabo, and manager Lou Piniella?

And what of those not on the field, like chatty, whimsical radio broadcaster Waite Hoyt, who regaled all of Ohio and Kentucky with his days-gone-by stories during rain delays? Or Powel Crosley, who bought the team in 1926 and saved it?

The sun sets over Riverfront Stadium in the third inning of this 1992 night game. The city's business district is just over the top tier of the stadium.

1912, was a classic early ballpark and had some of the game's greatest quirks, like the left and center outfields, which ran uphill, and the high left field wall, built just inches from a busy city street and a thriving laundry. Everything happened at Crosley. Pennants were won there four times. Two World Series were won there. In 1937, after a heavy storm that ravaged the Ohio River, the entire ballpark was flooded and players got around it in rowboats.

Cincinnati, more than most clubs, has had a long and strong tradition. Other teams were strong for fifty years and then weak. Some started off slowly and then were hot. The Reds could always be counted on to play good baseball, era after era. Most of all, though, they never abandoned their fans. The Reds never moved to another city because their hometown wouldn't build them a stadium or give them a tax break. They never even moved out of downtown. They have played baseball in Cincinnati, within a fly ball of the Ohio River, for 125 long years. Generation after generation of kids and adults has seen them play ball through hot summer days and cold April nights, in last place and first. They still play today for fans who first saw them on a warm and balmy spring evening long ago with *their* fathers, who first saw them with their fathers, who first saw them with their fathers. . . .

What about Schottzies I and II?

There was nothing inhuman or machinelike about any of them, and together they made baseball history. Cincinnati, of course, fielded the first professional team in the country, but it is remembered for more than that. The city was host to some of the prettiest ballparks in America, starting with League Park in the 1880s and 1890s, and then the Palace of the Fans, perhaps the most beautiful ballpark America has seen, at the turn of the century. Crosley Field, built as Redland Field in

13

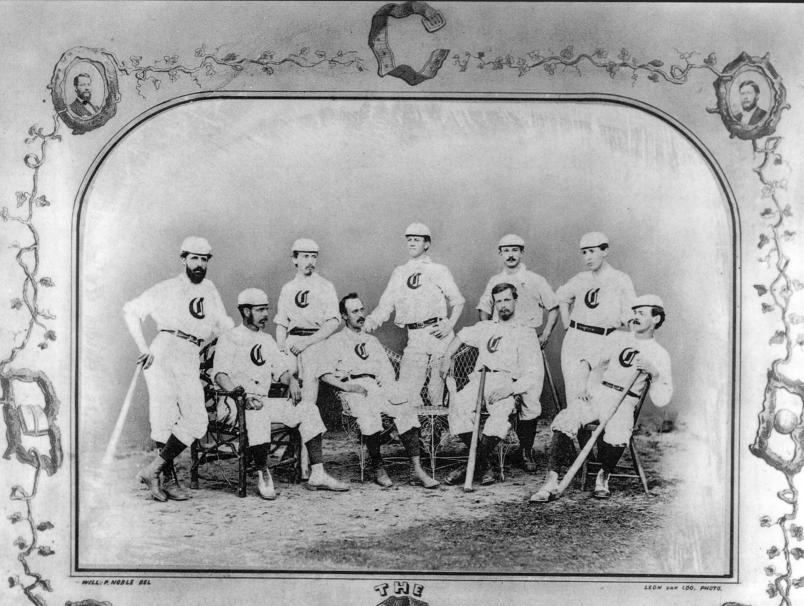

WILL. P. NOBLE DEL

LEON VAN LOO. PHOTO.

FIRST THE C THE NINE.

CHAPTER ONE

THE UNDEFEATED WONDERS

1860s–1899

A sprawling, raucous crowd of more than seven thousand New Yorkers jammed Union Grounds, one of just two enclosed wooden ballparks in the city, on a muggy summer afternoon in 1869, and four thousand more sat or stood on rooftops overlooking the outfield. Thousands of dollars had been gambled on the much-publicized game. Fistfights had broken out before and during it. The sale of beer had been brisk. Now, however, the fans watched the field, each concerned no doubt with his share of the money gambled on the contest. The game between the hometown Mutuals and the visiting Cincinnati Red Stockings was tied 2-2 in the ninth.

As Andrew Leonard, the Red Stockings' right fielder, passed third base in a wide swath and headed straight for home on a single to center field, the crowd rose as one large tidal wave of noise. Then, as he leaped into the air and landed on the plate for the winning run, the noise turned to a groan whose sound drifted through Brooklyn and over the East River to Manhattan.

When they lost that barn burner to the Red Stockings, the New York Mutuals—who had been called the best team in baseball—became just another victim, the seventeenth, of Cincinnati's unprecedented tour. The Red Stockings would go on to beat fifty-one more, with one

This 1869 Cincinnati squad was the nation's first all-professional team. The team went on an East Coast tour that was so successful that telegrams came into its Queen City office every day asking for games on the West Coast, so a California tour was added. The team never lost a game, garnered much publicity, and put baseball on the map.

15

This distinguished looking chap, in his best Sunday suit and carefully trimmed mustache, is John Ellard, captain of the Cincinnati Baseball Club's junior nine, a subsidiary of the professional team.

This remarkably preserved magazine page is a woodcut of the first professional team, the Cincinnati nine of 1869. It was a true "ringer" team, with players recruited from all over the country. A collection of all-stars, the team beat everybody in its coast to coast tour that summer.

284   FRANK LESLIE'S ILLUSTRATED NEWSPAPER.   [JULY 17, 1869.

GEORGE WRIGHT, SWEASY, HURLEY (Substitute).   WATERMAN.   LEONARD, HENRY WRIGHT.   BRAINARD.   GOULD, McVEY, ALLISON.

THE PICKED NINE OF THE CINCINNATI (RED STOCKINGS) BASE-BALL CLUB, OF CINCINNATI, OHIO.—FROM A PHOTOGRAPH BY F. L. HUTE.—SEE PAGE 279.

The echoes of Civil War cannon had not yet faded when in 1866 these four took over the reigns of the Cincinnati Baseball Club. Aaron Champion, top right, was the driving force of the club and later the professional team, giving up his lucrative law practice for two years to accompany it on its tour around the country.

controversial tie, by scores like 103-8 and 94-7, in the only undefeated season in the history of the game. Those who lost money on the game might not have cared at that moment, but they were witnessing the birth of a new era in baseball. The 1869 Red Stockings were the first all-professional team, with players on yearly salaries of $800 to $1,400. Until then, all of the teams in the United States were amateur clubs, whether they were gentlemen's sports clubs like the Knickerbockers in New York or blue-collar factory teams in Boston. Some hired a few professionals, but not many. The Red Stockings started as just another club in 1867, with most of its players coming from the 380 members of the totally amateur Cincinnati Baseball Club.

ALFRED T. GOSHORN,
President.

AARON B. CHAMPION,
Vice-President.

HENRY GLASSFORD,
Treasurer.

EDWARD E. TOWNLEY,
Secretary.

FIRST OFFICERS CINCINNATI BASEBALL CLUB, 1866.
From photos taken at the time.

The amateur Cincinnati Baseball Club wanted to go pro, so in 1867 they hired Harry Wright to do it. Wright, originally from England and a cricket star, was one of the game's finest managers already. Once in Cincinnati, he hired the best players in the country and in 1869 sent America's first all-pro baseball team on a national tour.

Baseball had been played on the banks of the Ohio River in the Queen City since the early 1850s, but grew in popularity after the Civil War. It was a popular game in army camps and all soldiers either played it or watched it. They brought it home to their cities, towns, and farms at the end of the war, planting the seeds that were to grow and make baseball the national pastime. Baseball was played all over Cincinnati and its neighbor across the river, Covington, Kentucky, and in other Ohio Valley towns after the Civil War.

17

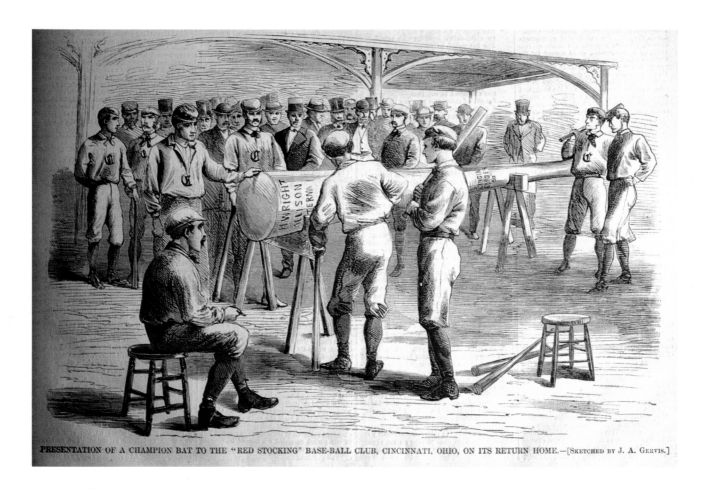

PRESENTATION OF A CHAMPION BAT TO THE "RED STOCKING" BASE-BALL CLUB, CINCINNATI, OHIO, ON ITS RETURN HOME.—[SKETCHED BY J. A. GERVIS.]

This woodcut from an 1869 issue of *Harper's Weekly* depicts the presentation of yet another honorary bat to the Reds on their triumphant, undefeated national tour.

There were more than forty different amateur teams. Young William Howard Taft played for the Auburn nine.

The biggest club was the Cincinnati Baseball Club, made up of prominent citizens and top athletes (many of them local lawyers). Harry Wright, a prominent ballplayer and cricket champion from Boston, signed on as team captain in 1867.

In 1868 Wright convinced the team to bring in four more professionals from different cities. In 1869 the club went completely professional, with talented players such as Charlie Gould, Fred Waterman, and Cal McVey, and built its own ballpark where Union Terminal now stands. Games were advertised in local newspapers with special promotions; tickets were twenty-five cents, payable in "shinplasters," the paper currency of the day. Thrilled with early success on the field and at the box office, the club arranged an eastern tour and, later, a tour of the West that carried them all the way to San Francisco. Now called the Red Stockings, from the bright red socks in their uniforms, the team traveled by boat, railroad, and even stagecoach to take on all comers in all the major cities and even such smaller ones as Omaha, Albany, and Louisville. The nine players, from six different cities, were practically an all-star team of the era. They had a club secretary who made certain the team got pregame publicity and a hefty percentage of the gate in tour cities and convinced the *Cincinnati Gazette* to send a reporter on tour with them to file stories each day for the folks back home. The club secretary

This photo captures the spirit of opening day at League Park in 1869. Players would walk along with carriages and floats as fans cheered. The park later burned down.

"Big Parade" opening day. 1869

CINCINNATIS.
CHAMPIONS 1882.
AMERICAN ASSOCIATION.

McCormick—P. Powers—C. Stearns—1st B. McPhee—2d B.
Carpenter—3d B. Snyder—C. White—P. Fulmer—S. S. Sommer—L. F.
Macullar—C. F. Wheeler—R. F.

Cincinnati certainly made a splash in 1882, when they went into the American Association and won the pennant in the league's first season. (The Reds had been booted out of the National League for selling beer at games.) Henry Carpenter, far left, hit .342. Will "Whoop La" White, the rather sour-looking pitcher seated in the middle, won forty games (he was the first pitcher to wear glasses).

The cover and pages of this ornate 1887 scorecard show how detailed and richly designed advertisements were at the end of the century. Note the fifty-cent round-trip fare on the steamboat and the twenty-five-cent tickets for the Peoples Theatre.

also telegraphed game results to an office in downtown Cincinnati, where hundreds of people would gather for the scores. As Cincinnati barnstormed the country, capacity crowds of five to twelve thousand turned out in cities across America to watch the local heroes take on the Cincinnati juggernaut.

The Red Stockings kept up their winning streak in early 1870, but in midseason finally lost a game in New York to the Atlantics, 4-2 (a New York fan ran out of the stands and tackled a fielder with the ball, enabling two runs to score), and then dropped several more. The team's president, Aaron Champion, traveling all spring and summer with no salary, quit at the end

of the season to return to his law office. Harry Wright was recruited to start a team in his hometown of Boston that spring and, feeling that the Cincinnati club was rudderless without Champion, he went back to Boston, taking his brother George (who hit .629 in 1869) and two other starters with him. In September, the rest of the Red Stockings followed him.

Back in Cincinnati, the Red Stockings' ballpark stood deserted for six years. The Cincinnati Baseball Club had been the strongest team in the city, and no other group had the players, organization, or finances to back a professional team.

The national tour of the Red Stockings and the enormous publicity they

21

received as an invincible team put the game of baseball squarely on the map, giving it instant notoriety. The Red Stockings also set a pattern for professional routines and behavior that would be the standard throughout baseball. The players had to meet a curfew, make trains and boats on time or risk fines, and attend regularly held practices, at home and away. The national tour proved that professional baseball was good baseball and that it could draw

This is one of the gorgeous scorecards sold in Cincinnati in 1888.

This old cabinet photo shows the 1888 Reds team during its eight-year sojourn in the American Association. The brightly painted white boards of **Findlay Park's grandstand are behind the squad. Despite having three pitchers who won twenty games each, the Reds finished fourth that year.**

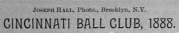

JOSEPH HALL, Photo., Brooklyn, N.Y.

CINCINNATI BALL CLUB, 1888.

1. Keenan.
2. J. G. Reilly.
3. Carpenter.
4. McPhee.
5. Corkhill.
6. Mullane.
7. Nicol.
8. Smith.
8. Fennelly.
10. Connor.
11. Viau.

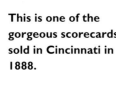

The 1888 Reds finished fourth in the American Association, but they probably had the sharpest-looking uniforms in the league. The team boasted three twenty-game winners (Viau, Mullane, and Smith). Aaron Stern, who owned the team for many years, is in the center, second row.

—✷CINCINNATI'S ✛ 1888.✶—

CORKHILL–M. F.		TEBEAU–L. F.		HART–P.		McPHEE–2ND B.		SERAD–P.		KAPPEL–3RD B.
MULLANE–P.	REILLY–1ST B.		GUS. SCHMELZ, MANAGER.		AARON STERN, PRESIDENT.		LOUIS HAUCK, SECRETARY.		KEENAN–C		VIAU–P
		SMITH–P.		FENNELLY–S. S.		NICOL–R. F.		BALDWIN–C.	

LEVI & GOLD.   166-168 W. FIFTH ST.

crowds. Its success put the idea of all-professional baseball teams into the heads of entrepreneurs from the Atlantic to the Mississippi River.

In 1871 the National Association of Professional Baseball Players was formed with several dozen teams from Mississippi to Maine. There were teams in just about every major city except Cincinnati. They played home and away games and tried to duplicate the success of the Red Stockings. The league had myriad problems, however. Players would jump from one team to another in midseason for higher pay. Teams short of cash would sometimes cancel weekend trips to another city. Gambling, even in the grandstands, was rampant, and several players were accused of fixing games. By 1876 the National Association was on the verge of collapse.

This 1893 scorecard was typical of the lavishly drawn cards of the day. The Reds finished seventh that year, one of the years the National League had 12 teams.

In that same year William Hulbert, owner of the Chicago White Stockings (the present-day Cubs), gathered men from several large cities at a meeting in New York. He was convinced that a "super" league of baseball teams could be successful. He and his colleagues picked the strongest National Association teams and added Cincinnati. The Queen City team joined Chicago, Louisville, and St. Louis in the Western Division, and teams from New York, Hartford, Boston, and Philadelphia made up the Eastern Division of what they called the National League, the very first major league.

The Cincinnati team, again called the Red Stockings, was owned by Josiah Koeck, a local meatpacker whose factory was at the stockyards. Across the way from his company he built Cincinnati Ballpark, a rectangular field with areas in the outfield where the rich could sit in their carriages and watch the game in comfort. Other fans could get there by using the Cincinnati & Marietta railroad, which charged fifteen cents for the ride from downtown, or the horse-drawn streetcars. The park, built on clay with little grass, had a three-thousand-seat wooden grandstand and two thousand more seats along the foul lines. Left field was lower than center and right fields and was sometimes flooded when the waters of nearby Mill Creek rose after a hard rain.

Koeck, who made sure all spectators could see his company and its sign from the seats (why build the ballpark there anyway?), charged fifty cents a ticket, as all National League teams did, but added a section called "Little Dukes," in front of the beer concession, where imbibers paid just ten cents. "No Gambling" signs were posted in each section. There was a "dressing room" for ladies under the stands, an effort by the team to attract women to what was a roughhouse game at the time. All games in the National League were played on Tuesdays, Thursdays, and Saturdays (no games were permitted on Sundays). A large wooden scoreboard listed inning-by-inning scores of the Red Stocking games as well as other games in the league.

The Red Stockings won their very first game, 2-1, before a sparse crowd. The news of the win in the next day's paper helped build the crowd for game two to more than three thousand with, surely,

How did they ever squeeze all of the 1896 Reds, who finished third that year, onto this promotional coin, the size of a quarter?

This was the rather elegantly illustrated front page of the opening day issue of the Cincinnati Tribune in the spring of 1895.

This lovely 1898 Reds schedule was printed on the back of a playing card and inserted into deck boxes as a promotion.

lots of Little Dukes. The Red Stockings won that one, too, 5-2. In the third game of the season, against the Chicago White Stockings, Chicago's Ross Barnes hit the first home run in National League history, an inside-the-park drive to left. In the very next inning the Red Stockings' center fielder, Charlie Jones, did even better, lofting a long, high drive over the left fielder, over the carriages, and off the wall. He, too, made it home for an inside-the-park homer. Nevertheless, the White Stockings ended up pounding the Red Stockings in that series, and the team never recovered, losing twenty-four of their next twenty-five games. At the end of the season they had a miserable record of nine wins and fifty-six losses, which would go down as the second worst record in National League history.

It was so bad that the *Cincinnati Commercial* newspaper ran editorials begging visiting teams to let the hapless Reds win. After announcing that there was a game that day and telling fans to go to the park "to see the Cincinnati Red Stockings Base Ball Club get their regular licking," the paper went on to implore: "Come, give us a chance, old fellows. We haven't had a good old fashioned baseball shriek in Cincinnati for weeks and weeks. Give us a game or two." No one obliged.

Left, the *Cincinnati Enquirer,* a supporter of the team throughout the struggling season of 1899, printed this schedule in April. Noodles Hahn won 23 for the Reds that year.

The Red Stockings were woeful in 1877, finishing last again despite the fine play of Lipman Pike, the first Jewish player in the majors. They moved into second place just once, in 1878, when Will White won thirty games and flamboyant Mike "King" Kelly made his debut. They placed fifth in 1879 and last again in 1880.

There may not have been many victories in those first few years, but there was always plenty of beer. Cincinnati's several breweries sold thousands of beers to fans at Cincinnati Ballpark, despite constant reprimands from the league, which had

outlawed beer at games. Finally, in 1880, after the team moved downtown to Bank Street Grounds, downtown, the issue of beer came to a head, and the league ordered the beer stands shut. Koeck refused, and Cincinnati was kicked out of the league.

There was no baseball in Cincinnati in 1881, but a new league, the American Association, came along in 1882 and offered fans four things: good baseball, good baseball on Sunday, good baseball for just a quarter, and good baseball with beer. Cincinnati signed right up. The Red

Pendleton Park was used for one season, 1891, by a new American Association team that challenged the Reds. Pendleton was isolated on the east end of town, and fans had to get there on steamships and trains. The lovely setting, right on the Ohio with the forested banks of Kentucky on the other side, made for great baseball, but the team folded in one year.

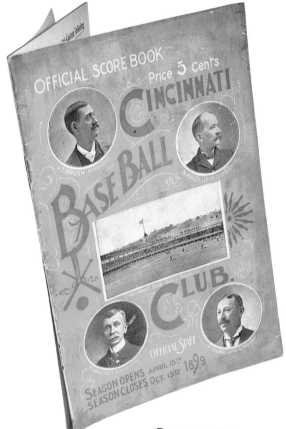

Department store mogul John Brush, top left, graces the cover of this 1899 score book. Much of the grandstand pictured in the center burned down in the off-season in 1900.

Stockings won the AA championship in 1882, and challenged National League champ Chicago to the first "World Series," a two-game affair in Cincinnati that ended in a draw. The team moved to League Park, at Findlay and Western, in 1884. Six years later, under the new ownership of businessman Aaron Stern, they rejoined the National League, which had softened its beer rules in 1890. The American Association folded after that season.

The last decade of the nineteenth century was not a good one for the Cincinnati club, now becoming simply as "the Reds." The best they could do was third in 1896 and 1898, despite hitters like Bid McPhee, Bug Holliday, Arlie Latham, and Jake Beckley (who hit over .300 in six of his seven seasons in Cincinnati), and pitchers Billy Rhines and Frank Foreman. The Reds also had William "Dummy" Hoy, a deaf mute who was also a fine hitter, batting .312 in 1894. Umpires invented hand signals for strikes and outs so that Hoy could understand their calls.

The team had two top skippers during those years. After a career as catcher with the New York Giants that would earn him a place in the Hall of Fame, William "Buck" Ewing took the reins in 1895 (that year he would take the Reds to their first spring training, in Mobile, Alabama). He followed young Charlie Comiskey, who

rebuilding would be needed. However, the new century began on a scale of ominous notes. Just before the start of the 1900 season, the grandstands at League Park burned to the ground. That tragedy was followed by one of the greatest blunders in baseball history: The Reds managed to secure a young pitcher just up from the minors who had been rejected by the Giants and then traded him back to the Giants because they didn't think he was any good. The kid's name was Christy Mathewson.

There have been many home plate weddings in ballparks across the country, but the marriage of Reds groundskeeper Louie Rapp in 1895 was one of the loveliest.

Harry Ellard's 1907 volume on the history of baseball in Cincinnati has become a collector's treasure. Its first commercial printing was of more than five thousand copies, but this first commemorative edition is one of just five hundred.

played several seasons for the Reds and then began his long and distinguished career as a manager of several ball clubs. Comiskey left Cincinnati in 1894 to work with his friend Ban Johnson, who had just started the Western Association.

The year 1899 was a disaster for the Reds. Bid McPhee, who had played ball in town all his life, retired, and Buck Ewing quit as manager. The team, then owned by department-store mogul John Brush, tumbled into last place.

After having practically invented professional baseball in the middle of the nineteenth century with the unbeatable squad of 1869, the Cincinnati team had steadily deteriorated on the field, even while organized baseball grew into an institution in Cincinnati and across the nation. Much

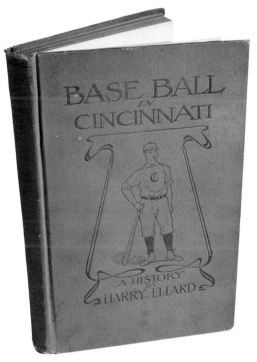

CHAPTER TWO

BUILDINGS AND REBUILDINGS
1900–1918

Ballparks at the turn of the century stood like big old barns in large American cities, the wind whistling through their open spaces in winter and their thin wooden walls creaking and their light roofs swaying in the March wind. They were designed to do little more than support a lot of seats so that the owners could sell a lot of tickets. The purpose of outfield walls was to be painted over with colorful and revenue-producing advertising signs as well as circle the outfield. Most stadiums were all wood, of a drab and lifeless design, and had one tier of seats and few amenities for fans. Even the best, like West Side Grounds in Chicago, were little more than two-tiered structures held together with unattractive and badly spaced wooden poles.

The Reds played the 1900 and 1901 seasons (they were fifth and last, respectively) at charred League Park, using temporary seats and a makeshift grandstand and roof. While the team stumbled, the owners took another look at the pictures they brought back from the 1893 World's Fair in Chicago. Intrigued by the stunning classical architecture of the buildings, they decided that if it looked good on Greek temples, why not on ballparks?

And so, in April 1902 League Park was reopened and promptly dubbed the "Palace of the Fans" by sportswriters, who were as awed by

When the Reds' ballpark burned down, the owners asked an architect to build a stadium with Roman architecture to resemble the style they fell in love with at the 1893 world's fair in Chicago. The result was one of the nation's prettiest ballparks, the Palace of the Fans. It had three tiers of seating, ample concessions, and it put fans very close to the field. Unfortunately, the Palace burned down ten years later.

31

The graphic designer of the Reds' lush 1900 score book was an optimist. Not only did the team fail to win the championship, as it says at the bottom, but it finished second to last.

playing area. In the middle of it all, as grand as the Temple of Dionysus, was a facade with a triangular pediment and *CINCINNATI* etched in large letters on the frieze. The Palace of the Fans was baseball's Parthenon.

This was no Golden Age on the field, though. Cincinnati seemed in a perennial slump in the standings. From 1902, when the Palace of the Fans opened, until 1919 the team never did better than third, and attendance never pushed much beyond five thousand a game.

The team did achieve an amazing amount of stability in those years, though. Since there was no Player's League team in Cincinnati, the cut-throat competition seen in 1890 was avoided. The new American Association team in town went out of business when the Player's League did. A major challenge came along in 1901, however. Ban Johnson, the former sportswriter who was head of the Western Association, founded the American League, whose teams, with their well-heeled owners, were an immediate threat to all National League teams in the cities where they played. In some, such as Boston, the American League team was so successful that the National franchise later moved out of town. Again, Cincinnati was unscathed. The American League saw Cincinnati as a small market and went after

the architectural wonder as everyone else. The "Palace" was the second concrete-and-steel stadium in America. It featured a huge, two-tiered main grandstand that swept from home plate to beyond first and third bases. The wooden grandstand, designed to resemble a Greek temple, had hundreds of intricately carved designs on its facade and dozens of ornately hand-carved Corinthian columns supporting the second deck and roof. A narrow tier of semicircular boxes, similar to Italian opera-house boxes, jutted out over the

These silver season passes were common among teams at the turn of the century. They cost more, but they were a symbol of wealth, like a 1990s Porsche, flaunted by their owners.

This 1901 pass got the bearer into the ballpark. In those days there was no numbered seating, and fans sat wherever they wanted. Men complained bitterly that on ladies' day the women arrived early to grab the best seats.

This rather elegant invitation was to opening day for the first season at the Palace of the Fans, the Reds glamorous new ballpark built to look like an old Greek or Roman temple.

cities like Chicago, Detroit, Boston, and New York instead.

In 1902 the Reds' owner John Brush bought the Giants and sold the Reds to a local quartet consisting of Julius and Max Fleischman, of the gin and yeast family; political boss George Box; and Garry Hermann, president of the city's waterworks commission. The other three let Hermann run the team. It was a wise decision for the team and for baseball. Hermann, a heavyset man with a trim moustache and hair neatly parted in the middle, was a well-dressed, genial, outgoing executive who was as much the fans' owner as the players'. He saw baseball as entertainment as well as sport and was a familiar figure striding through the stands shaking hands and conversing with fans. He quickly became one of the most respected people in the game, so respected that in 1903, when a three-man commission was formed to make peace between the warring National and American leagues, baseball executives asked Hermann to join it, along with the presidents of each league.

33

CROSLEY FIELD

Crosley Field (Redland Field in its debut) was the Taj Mahal of ballparks when it was built in 1912 at Western Avenue and Findlay Street, the site of the previous four Reds ballparks, all of which burned down. It was a large stadium for its time—two tiers, twenty-eight thousand seats—in an era of seven-thousand-person crowds. Its owners, though, like the owners of the Giants, Cubs, and Red Sox, who all built large new stadiums in the same era, had a vision of baseball drawing twenty-five thousand and more to ball games.

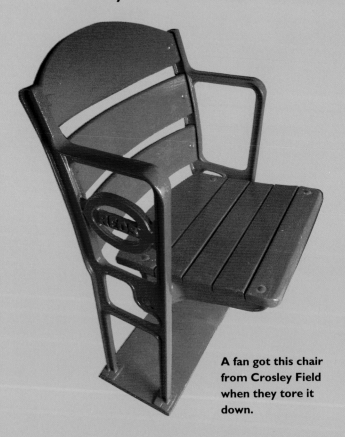

A fan got this chair from Crosley Field when they tore it down.

When it opened, Crosley had the largest field in the big leagues, with center field 420 feet from home, and the left and right field walls at 360 feet. It was shoehorned into a busy neighborhood of stores, homes, and factories (the Young and Bertke Sheet Metal factory and a large laundry were behind the right field fence, the Lackner Neon Signs plant behind center, and the Standard Electric Tool Company behind left). The field was larger than the previous fields on the site, but the outfield sloped upward at about thirty degrees. The fans loved Redland because the seats were extremely close to the field and they could hear players talking to each other in the dugouts and hear the chatter between players and umpires, batters and catchers.

"You sat so close that when a guy slid into home plate the dust would come down in your lap," said Bob Long, who grew up with the Reds

This recent lithograph depicts a 1950s game at Crosley. If you look carefully, you can see how the outfield slopes up toward the fences.

This was one of the five-foot-long, three-foot-high heavy metal signs that hung over ticket booths to advertise prices.

ALL BOX SEATS $3.00

$2.50 RESERVED SEATS

GENERAL ADMISSION $1.50

$2.00 LADIES BOX SEATS

LADIES RESERVED SEATS $1.50

50¢ LADIES GENERAL ADMISSION

ABOVE PRICES INCLUDE ALL TAXES

These two locker tags were taken from the home locker room at Crosley the day it closed.

CROSLEY FIELD LOCKER NO. 20 CINCINNATI REDS

CROSLEY FIELD LOCKER NO. 5 CINCINNATI REDS

Two complete tickets from the last game every played at Crosley Field.

M y mother took me every ladies' day when I was a kid. She would dress up like she was going to church and behave very, very ladylike until her hero, Ivy Goodman came to bat. Then she'd go wild, jumping up and down, waving her hat in the air, and continually yelling "Hit the laundry, Goody, hit the laundry!"

—JERRY SCHWERTMAN, FIFTY-FOUR

T he ballpark's closeness brought the fans into the game. In big parks the fans were far away, like little dots, but at Crosley they were right on top of you, big as life. You weren't just playing for some anonymous group of people. You were playing for them and you knew who they were. You could see their faces, talk to them between innings. It was a great feeling.

—JOE NUXHALL

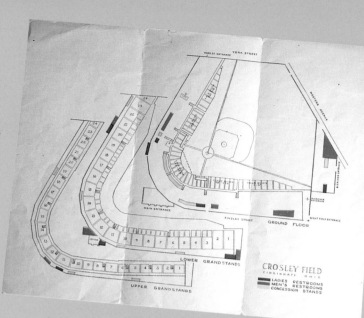

This is the architect's rendering of the stadium, given to fans so they could find their seats.

This oversize, eight-foot-high championship flag hung at Crosley for years.

Before the '61 World Series Casey [Stengel], who played there a lot, had us practice running up and down and sideways on the hills in the outfield for an hour each day. It was the craziest park I ever saw—you had to be a billy goat to play it.

MOOSE SKOWRON OF THE YANKEES.

The Reds always dressed in style and so did the ushers at the ballpark.

in Cincinnati. The players loved it, too, because it gave them a sense of being part of the city and the crowd.

In 1934, when Powel Crosley, Jr., bought the team, Redland Field was renamed Crosley Field. It was home to winning efforts in the World Series in 1919 (the notorious "Black Sox" Series) and 1940 and losing ones in 1939 and 1961. Crosley was the site of major-league baseball's first night game in 1935 and of several championship boxing bouts, too.

Over its fifty-eight years it was sometimes

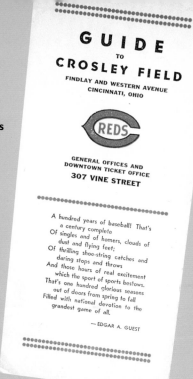

These guides to Crosley could be tucked into a fan's pocket.

GUIDE
TO
CROSLEY FIELD
FINDLAY AND WESTERN AVENUE
CINCINNATI, OHIO

REDS

GENERAL OFFICES AND
DOWNTOWN TICKET OFFICE
307 VINE STREET

A hundred years of baseball! That's
a century complete
Of singles and of homers, clouds of
dust and flying feet;
Of thrilling shoo-string catches and
daring stops and throws
And those hours of real excitement
which the sport of sports bestows.
That's one hundred glorious seasons
out of doors from spring to fall
Filled with national devotion to the
grandest game of all.

—EDGAR A. GUEST

Fan Willie DeLuca managed to get one of these seats from Crosley. Pete Rose signed it for him.

jammed past capacity, as it was in the 1919 World Series when extra bleachers were built on top of the left-field wall and five thousand people were seated in the outfield. At other times it was practically vacant, as it was in the 1930s, when less than a thousand fans would show up for a game. Some things never changed. The kids in the knot-hole gangs always sat in the right field pavilion, radio personality Dick Bray (WSAI) always did his "Fans in the Stands" program from the bleachers, Tuesday was always ladies' day, and the streetcar always took too long to get there.

By 1970 the neighborhood around Crosley had decayed, and the stadium's age had caught up with it. A brand-new ballpark, Riverfront Stadium, opened downtown on the banks of the river. All that's left at the corner of Western and Findlay now are ghosts.

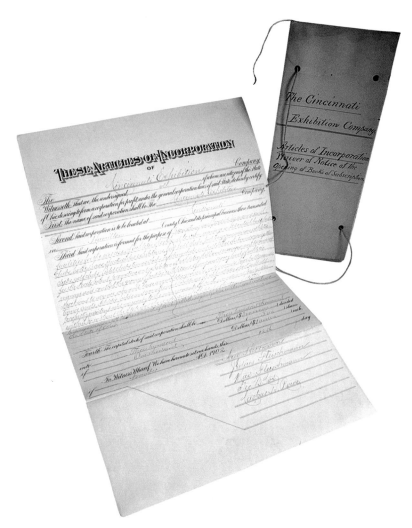

These are the actual papers of incorporation filed by John T. Brush, owner of the Reds, when he sold the team in 1902. Brush then bought the New York Giants.

The conflict between the two leagues hurt many National League teams, but actually benefited the Reds because the competition caused many top National League players to become free agents of sorts, and the Reds picked up two full-blown stars, Cy Seymour and Joe Kelley, who had bolted from the Baltimore team.

They were two of the many fine players in Cincinnati in the first decade of the century. Seymour hit .340 in the second half of 1902 and hit a thumping .377 in 1905. Kelley hit .321 in 1902; Jake Beckley hit .330. In fact, the Reds' .282 team average was second best in the league that year. On the mound, Frank "Noddles" Hahn won twenty-two games with an impressive 1.76 ERA.

In 1903 Hahn won twenty-two games again, Seymour hit .342, and Harry Steinfeldt hit .312. That was the year of the first World Series, one of the successes of the new national commission and the peace treaty. One of the more glaring failures was the confusion that ended the Reds career of Wahoo Sam Crawford.

Crawford was a raw nineteen years old, six feet tall and full of muscle, when he came to the Reds in 1899. He played thirty games at the end of the season and hit .307. The left-handed slugger, famous for long fly balls that often went over fences, hit over .300 in 1900 and .335 in 1901 (with a record sixteen home runs). He was one of the game's true stars, showing such promise that the Detroit Tigers, a new American League entry, wooed him at the end of the 1902 season and signed him to a contract. Crawford then signed with the Reds again in the

The box score for a 1903 game against Philadelphia shows that Cy Seymour went two for five and Joe Kelley (the paper misspelled his name) two for four. Both players sizzled that season—Seymour hit .342 and Kelley .316—but the team came in fourth.

Right, in 1902, August (Gerry) Hermann was the waterworks commissioner for Cincinnati. When a triumvirate of local businessmen bought the team, they asked Hermann to come along as a partner and run the team as president. He agreed and quickly became one of the most influential forces in baseball. He ran the team through the good years and bad until 1927, when he resigned due to failing health.

spring of 1903, convinced his Detroit contract meant nothing in lieu of the peace treaty. If he had had more pens, who knows how many contracts Crawford would have signed? After a bitter debate, the American and National League chiefs, seeing Crawford as a way to smooth things over politically between the two leagues, voted against Hermann, Crawford's employer, and awarded him to the Tigers. Sam Crawford went on to make the Hall of Fame as he hit a record 312 triples to go with ninety-seven home runs and 1,525 RBIs. He would hit cleanup behind Ty Cobb at Detroit, and they would take the team to pennants in 1907, 1908, and 1909.

As the Reds struggled in those early years Hermann tried a number of man-

agers, all of whom did nothing for the Reds but had been stars somewhere else or would go on to be stars somewhere else. Ned Hanlon kept the Reds in the second division in 1906 and 1907; he had taken Brooklyn to a pennant earlier. Next was young Clark Griffith, who took the Reds to fourth in 1909, fifth in 1910, and sixth in 1911; he later became owner of

Cy Seymour was a horse, six feet tall and 200 pounds. He came to the Reds from Baltimore, then in the American League, in the middle of the 1902 season and hit a league-leading .377 in 1905. In an early blockhead trade, Seymour was sent back to the Giants in 1906.

the Washington Senators. Then there were Henry O'Day, Hall of Famer Joe Tinker, and Christy Mathewson, all of whom were very good at telling stories about the good old days but very bad at managing. Buck Herzog managed to hang on for three seasons, but the team never finished better than seventh under him.

Players came and went. The good ones mostly went. Cy Seymour, who Hermann thought was washed up, was

shipped to the Giants, where he averaged .308 in three of his four seasons. Harry Steinfeldt was sent to the Cubs, whom he helped to a world championship with a club leading batting average in 1908. There were men who didn't make it on or off the field. Larry McLean came in as a six-foot, five-inch catcher who drank steins of beer nearly as big as he was. Constantly in trouble, he was suspended once after he got into a brawl with John McGraw in a hotel (McGraw broke a chair over his head). In 1921, following an argument, a Boston bartender shot him to death.

There were bright moments in those years, and there were eventful seasons, such as the season of 1911. That was the spring the Reds set an all-time scoring record when they beat the Boston Braves 26-3. That same year they became the first major league team to hire Cubans, when they signed on Armando Marsans and Rafael Almeida. The two men played well, and Marsans led the Reds in hitting the next season. (Hundreds of outstanding black players hoped the hiring of the Cubans, both of whom were light skinned, would open the door to the National and American leagues for them, but it did not.) The 1911 season ended on a sour note, when the gorgeous Palace of the Fans burned down.

Every single Red in Cincinnati was shown in this unique 1909 schedule fans could put on their walls.

Cincinnati took a major step forward as the Greek temple stadium still smoldered. Like most ballparks of the era, the Palace had seated only about seven thousand people. Hermann was convinced that baseball was growing (teams in Chicago and New York were selling twelve thousand tickets a game), and had a vision of baseball games attracting three, four, five times as many people. Accordingly, he built Redland Field, a huge twenty-eight-thousand-seat, two-tiered steel-and-cement stadium. Redland, on the site of the Palace, had the largest playing field in baseball, with center field 420 feet away and deep foul poles. It also had baseball's wildest outfield. Because the old field had to be expanded over rocky terrain, the last sixty feet of the outfield ran uphill. Fans loved Redland because the stands were built

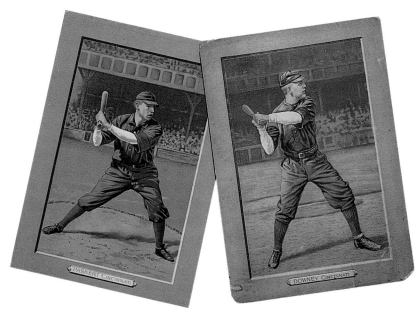

Tom Downey and Dode Paskert appeared on these Turkey Red baseball cards distributed in 1910. Paskert hit .300 that year and Downey .270.

tight against the field and the sight lines were wonderful. Perhaps best of all, to fill the twenty-eight thousand seats for a second division club the Reds started numerous knothole gangs, ticket clubs, and promotional giveaways.

Having built a new ballpark, Hermann set to work on rebuilding the team. In six years, he would have world champions. It all began in 1912 when, with little fanfare, the Reds acquired third baseman Heine Groh, who hit line drives with his strangely shaped "bottle bat."

The rebuilding had its fits and starts. Sometimes the wrong players were signed. In the spring of 1914, a Cincinnati scout

Crosley Field was one of the country's grand old ballparks and served as home to the Reds for 58 years.

The top two pins here were found in cigarette boxes around 1910. Hartnett's pin came out of a Crackerjacks box in the 1930s.

This issue of *Sporting Life* chronicled the slow starts of both Chicago teams as the 1910 season began.

went to watch the Baltimore Orioles, then playing in the International League. He was impressed with two players, whom he signed—Claud Derrick, who would go on to play just thirty games in 1914 and hit .225 before being let go, and George Twombly, who would play an average of only thirty games a year in five major league seasons, hit .211, and retire. One player the scout did not think much of and did not sign was a young pitcher named Babe Ruth.

Sometimes good players came but didn't stick. Hal Chase, a veteran of the Federal League, was signed by the Reds in 1915 and hit .339. His production dwindled in subsequent years, and he went to the Giants in 1919. In 1917 Olympic great

and later football star Jim Thorpe joined the team. After seventy-seven games, Thorpe, too, went to the Giants.

Fred Toney came in 1917 and left in 1918, but in the meantime he made it into the record books. Toney was an inconsistent pitcher whose record was 15-6 in 1915 but 6-10 in 1918. He later soared to 21-11 and 18-11 years with the Giants, but also had several losing seasons. He seemed to be up or down. On the afternoon of May 2, 1917, he was up. He pitched a no-hitter against the Cubs. It did him little good, however, because Jim "Hippo" Vaughn of the Cubs also threw a no-hitter. The two men carried their battle into the tenth inning. In that final stanza, the Reds finally touched Vaughn for a single. A dropped fly

43

Like Joe Tinker in Chicago, Edd Roush not only had lots of fans, but his very own cigar box.

think he had a future after he hit .188 in two months with the club.

With the Reds Roush was a sensation right away. He hit .287 in sixty-nine games with Cincinnati in 1916, but won the National League batting title in 1917 with a .341 average and won it again in 1919 with .321. In his first eleven seasons in the league the center fielder, who used a very heavy, thick-handled bat, hit over .300, with a .352 average in 1921 and .351 in 1923. He finished with a career average of .323. In the field, he was just as good. Like Tris Speaker in the American League, he seemed to have a sixth sense about where a ball would go. As quick as a cat, he would grab line drives just over second base or race back to the wall to snatch a long fly ball. Although managers, players, and fans loved him, the front office was exasperated with Roush because he constantly held out for more money on his contracts, one time missing half a season and another time an entire year because of his demands.

By 1919, the hitting of Groh and Roush had been complemented by the additions of Jake Daubert, obtained in a trade from Brooklyn, Larry Kopf, catcher Ivy Wingo, and outfielder Greasy Neale. (The multi-talented Neale would go on to coach the Philadelphia Eagles to the NFL championship in 1949.)

ball put runners on first and third, and the lone run scored when Thorpe hit a slow roller to third. Vaughn took it and fired home to get Chase, but the Cubs catcher dropped the ball. Toney held the Cubs hitless in the tenth, winning the only double no-hitter in baseball history.

Although some players didn't pan out, before long several others did. In 1916 by sheer chance the Reds acquired Edd Roush from the Giants, who did not

A fine pitching staff was patched together by trades that didn't look that good on paper. Slim Sallee came to the Reds on waivers from the Giants, where he had a mediocre 8-8 record. The team grabbed Ray Fisher from the Yankees, where he pitched just 8-9 in 1917 before going in the army in 1918. Dutch Ruether and Jimmy Ring had been on the team since 1917 but had accomplished little. Ring had records of 3-7 in 1917 and 9-5 in 1918. Ruether was 3-2 in 1917 and joined the army in 1918. From Cuba came rookie Dolf Luque, who would lead the league in shutouts three times in his career.

At last, the parts of the first Big Red Machine had been assembled.

Bats of Edd Roush (top) are hard to find, and the unusual "bottle bats" of Heine Groh almost impossible.

Groh holds his famous "bottle bat." The specially designed bat, with a long, thick barrel and extra long and thin handle, worked for Groh, but not others. A collector with a long memory picked up this plaque thanking Groh for his long service to little league baseball.

IN APPRECIATION FOR SERVICE TO BASEBALL AND YOUTH

HEINE GROH

ST. PETERSBURG BOOSTER CLUB FEB. 4, 1961.

CHAPTER THREE

HOLLOW VICTORY, DRY SEASONS
1919–1933

In tiny Waxahachie, Texas, where the Reds went for spring training in March 1919, it rained on Monday. It rained on Tuesday, Wednesday, Thursday, and Friday, too. It rained so hard on Saturday and Sunday that the Reds' ballpark there was flooded. It remained underwater as more rain, sometimes sheets of it, came down on Texas in that chilly March. The new skipper was Pat Moran, who had moved over from the staggering Phillies. He replaced Christy Mathewson, who had been gassed in World War I and was unable to work (the gas would kill him in 1925). At the end of the second week, when the rain stopped, it was clear that the flooded field was useless. Moran had his players work out in vacant lots, railroad yards, and even a local cemetery.

It was an ominous note; imagine how startled fans were, then, when the Reds, lacking any real preseason practice, won their first seven games, vaulting into first place. On May 11, Hod Eller tossed a no-hitter against the Cardinals. A team that had never even come within the shadow of first place since 1876 was now sprinting out in front of the National League. What was going on?

The start of the 1919 season proved to be no fluke, and with Roush's league-leading .321 batting average, and Sallee winning twenty-one games, veteran Hod Eller twenty, Ruether nineteen, and Fisher

Jake Daubert was one of baseball's most consistent hitters and one of its most tragic. He hit .300 or better ten years, had a .990 fielding average for fifteen years, and twice led the league in triples. He was traded from Brooklyn to the Reds after a salary dispute in 1919 and helped lead them to the world championship. In 1922, at the age of 38, he had 205 hits and batted .336 but died suddenly that winter following an appendectomy.

This souvenir book was one of the most handsome ever produced. Inside were pictures of each player in uniform and jacket and tie. A diamond-shaped cutout in the thick, heavy cover reveals a picture of Pat Moran on the next page. A full page of facsimile autographs of all the players (right) also appeared in it.

led by the best pure hitter in baseball history, Shoeless Joe Jackson (his .356 lifetime mark would rank third best).

Just before the infamous series began rumors started to fly that something funny was going on because enormous sums of money were being bet on the underdog Reds. Chicago started off as a clear favorite, with Jackson and Eddie Collins (.309) in the lineup and perhaps the two best pitchers in baseball, Eddie Cicotte (29-7) and Lefty Williams (23-11). The

A score book from the bittersweet 1919 season.

fourteen, the Reds took the pennant by nine games over the Giants. (Their fans also set an attendance record in a 140-game season shortened for fear of a post-war economic slump). In October, they braced for the best-of-nine World Series against the Chicago White Sox, who were

48

William M. Schmitt wrote one of the many Reds songs published over the years. Today old song sheets are prized by collectors, even if the music is forgettable.

same basic lineup and mound staff had won the World Series over the power-house Giants in 1917.

Despite the persistent rumors, Cincinnati gleefully braced itself for its first World Series. Hotels were full, extra trains were scheduled to bring fans in from Chicago, newspapers put out special edi-

tions, there were parties up and down the riverfront, and entrepreneurs produced special booklets and photo albums. Anticipating a sellout for each game, the Reds constructed a makeshift bleacher section behind the left field wall. Thousands of fans were permitted to sit in the rear of the outfield, a common prac-

PHOTO BY
C.J. BURNELL
HORNELL, N.Y.

"CINCINNATI" REDS

This long, thin photo of the 1919 National League champion Reds was similar to many team pictures taken with the predecessor of the wide-angle camera lens. The camera shutter clicked so slowly that players on the far left sometimes ran around behind the cameraman and stood on the far right quick enough to appear in the same picture twice.

tice of the day (fly balls into the crowd there were ground-rule doubles). Flags flew everywhere in Cincinnati in celebration of the city's first World Series.

Eddie Cicotte signaled the gamblers that the fix was on when he deliberately hit the first Reds batter, Morrie Rath. The Reds went on to win that game, 9-1, on some easy pitching and shoddy fielding by the White Sox. The Reds "won" game two 4-2. The White Sox players who were reportedly in on the fix included Swede Risberg, Cicotte, Williams, Fred McMullin, Chick Gandil, Hap Felsch, and Jackson (although his legion of supporters dispute that). All except Jackson made obvious errors or played cautiously (Jackson played

as hard as ever, hitting .375 for the series and cracking the only home run).

Sox pitcher Dickie Kerr was not in on the fix and he won game three, 3-1, despite the bungling behind him. The Reds won game four, 2-0, as the White Sox made some glaring errors. The Reds won game five, 5-0, with Eller the winner, as Hap Felsch booted some easy chances in the outfield. Kerr hurled game six and won. The White Sox then won game seven with Cicotte on the mound, confusing the gamblers. Were they really trying to win the series at the last hour, despite the fix? No one ever found out. The Sox let the Reds win game eight by the embarrassing score of 10-5. Cincinnati had won

NATIONAL LEAGUE CHAMPIONS. 1919

COPYRIGHT APPLIED FOR

its first world championship. There was joy in the streets, drinking in the speakeasies, and celebrating in small towns throughout Ohio. It was a moment that should have been treasured forever—but was treasured for just one year.

That's when the seven White Sox players (plus Buck Weaver, who did not participate but reputedly knew about it and told no one), dubbed the "Black Sox" by the press, were indicted for throwing the World Series. White Sox owner Charles Comiskey had been suspicious of the loss and had ordered an investigation. When it became apparent to the owners that something may have been going on, they decided to hire baseball's first commissioner, Judge

A newspaper cartoonist completed a series of caricature-style drawings of Reds and White Sox players that were published just before they clashed in the 1919 World Series. This was one.

REDS

CHAMPION

Ticket demand was so great for the 1919 World Series that management built extra bleachers over the street (shown here over the left field wall) and let thousands sit in the outfield.

A lucky fan kept this ticket stub from the third game of the controversial 1919 World Series, the "Black Sox" series, in which seven players on the White Sox took money to throw the series. Ironically, Chicago won game three, 3-0, on the arm of pitcher Dickie Kerr, who was not in on the fix.

The *Cincinnati Times-Star* editors were so jubilant over the 1919 world championship they put out a special edition to celebrate.

Reds' players hoist the world championship flag on the flagpole in center-field. Joy turned to sourness a year later, when it was revealed that the Series was fixed.

Kenesaw Mountain Landis, to oversee the investigation. But after the indictment the players' signed confessions—some of which had been made without a lawyer present—mysteriously disappeared from the police evidence room. Without them the state had no case, and the men were acquitted. Furious, and certain they were guilty, Commissioner Landis banned the eight from baseball for life anyway.

Justice may have been served, but it tarnished the World Series win for Groh, Roush, and the rest of the hard-playing Reds of 1919, who deserved better than to wind up as the answer to a trivia question.

The convoys of trucks that delivered cases of beer to Redland Field stopped running in 1919. The ballpark, renowned for its beer sales (remember, the Reds had quit the National League earlier because of a beer ban), was as dry as the rest of the nation when Prohibition went into effect. There were no more "Little Dukes"; the beer stands were ghost towns as the 1920s unfolded. After a promising start, so was the lineup of the Reds.

Like so many great teams the Reds stumbled the very year after their series win, finishing third, ten games back. Several of the pitchers were traded in early 1921

Now that so many years have gone by, Reds fans appreciate the great 1919 ball club, led by hard-hitting Jake Daubert, seated, far left.

THE CINCINNATI REDS – 1919

CINCINNATI REDS 1919 CHAMPIONS.
TOP ROW – ELLER, BRESSLER, MITCHELL, ROUSH, GROH, LUQUE, NEALE.
MIDDLE ROW – SALLEE, RUETHER, GERNER, RING, FISHER, RATH, DUNCAN, WINGO, KOPF.
LOWER ROW – DAUBERT, SMITH, Mgr.MORAN, SEE, SH.MAGEE,SCHREIBER,RARIDEN,ALLEN.

BOELLINGER CINCINNATI O.

Copyright Applied

Pitcher Ray Fisher, center, anchors this display of baseball photos that fans could buy from vending machines in the 1920s. The other players are, left to right, Morris Rath, Ivy Wingo, Rube Bressler, Eddie Gerner, Jimmy Smith, and Hank Schreiber.

and the team fell even further, down to sixth. In 1922 Hermann, eager for the Reds to get back to the series and vindicate themselves in a legitimate contest, acquired George Burns, Ike Caveney, and Babe Pinelli, and he brought up George Harper from the minors. That season the Reds hit a husky .296, with Harper at .340; Daubert, .336; Pinelli, .305. Lou Fonseca, up for eighty-one games, hit .361. Roush hit .352, but only played the last half of the season after another salary holdout. The pitching was sensational, helping the team finish second. Rookie Peter Donohue pitched 18-9.

The star of the pitching staff, though,

was the flamboyant Eppa Rixey. This six-foot-five-inch giant was murder on batters and, when he lost, murder on clubhouse furniture. In an era when most players never went to college, Rixey came into baseball straight from graduation at the University of Virginia, where he had earned a degree in chemistry. He had four lackluster years in Philadelphia before a new manager, Pat Moran, brought out his talents. He developed a wide array of pitches and, despite playing with many mediocre teams, compiled a 266-251 record (he made the Hall of Fame in 1963). Rixey was erratic. He won twenty-two games in 1916, but then lost twenty-

These postcards of the Reds ballparks over the years are often found at flea markets and make marvelous pieces of memorabilia.

one in 1917. He fought with the army in World War I. In 1921 Hermann snared him in a trade. The big hurler won twenty games three times in Cincinnati, with a high of twenty-five in 1922. He stayed with the Reds through 1933 and then retired to run an insurance company. He never did become a chemist.

The 1923 Reds team, which finished second, was one of the best ever. Roush, who decided to play all summer, hit .351. Luque had one of the finest seasons of any

pitcher, winning twenty-seven and posting a spartan ERA of 1.93.

If 1922 and 1923 were seasons of hope, 1924 was a season of tragedy. As soon as manager Moran got off the train in Orlando, Florida for spring training the players knew he was desperately ill. Moran died a few weeks later at age forty-eight. Coach Jack Hendricks replaced Moran and, despite little experience at the helm, did a fine job of guiding the mourning Reds to a creditable fourth place finish. They

Eppa Rixey, a tall, reed-thin pitcher with a whirlwind windup, pitched in the National League for twenty-one long years. He came to the Reds in 1921 after eight mediocre seasons with the Phillies, but blossomed on the banks of the Ohio, winning twenty or more games in three of the next five seasons. Rixey started often and while he won a lot, he lost a lot. Lifetime, he won 266, Hall of Fame numbers, but he also dropped 251.

didn't have time to celebrate the season, though, because just a week after it ended Jake Daubert died following a routine appendectomy. All of Cincinnati mourned.

In 1925 the team climbed the ladder to third, and in 1926 did better yet. That year they were in first place by midseason, when they stumbled. A month-long slump dropped them out of first, but it ended in mid-August, and by the first week of September they were back in first, though just barely. When there were only nine games to go in the season they shared first with St. Louis. The bubble burst on a road trip right after that, though, and the Reds stumbled back to Redland Field at the end of the season in second.

Even so, it was a season of outstanding performances. Donohue won twenty games, Mays nineteen, and Rixey fourteen. The hitters were even better. Catcher Bubbles Hargrave won the league batting title with a .353 mark, and two other hitters hit over .350. One of them was the mysterious Walter "Cuckoo" Christensen, who may have been the world's fastest-growing and quickest-forgotten legend. Cuckoo spent several uneventful seasons in the minors and was finally called up to the parent club as a twenty-seven-year-old rookie. He got into 114 games and stunned fans by hitting .350, second best in the league. In 1927 he played in only fifty-

The temperamental Edd Roush always held out for more money, once missing an entire season, 1930, in a salary dispute. He was the best centerfielder of his era and a consistent batsman who hit .300 eleven years in a row.

seven games and was let go. He drifted over the Ohio River and never played a major-league game again.

Reds fans were certain the red-hot 1926 club could bring another pennant back to the Queen City in 1927. That was a banner year in America. Ruth hit his sixty home runs and Lindbergh crossed the Atlantic. It was a long year in Cincinnati, though, where everything fell apart.

Gerry Hermann, the popular president, resigned because of failing health (he would die four years later). One of his last official acts was to finally get rid of Edd Roush and his contractual holdouts by

trading him. Luque and Rixey had subpar seasons in 1927, Donohue finished with a horrendous 6-16 record, and Bubbles Hargrave was the only player to hit .300. The Reds fell to fifth. In 1928 they were fifth again, then seventh in 1929, the year Dolf Luque departed. Luque had been the last link to the ill-fated team of 1919. That era was over; it would be up to a later generation of Reds to gain vindication.

In 1930 Sidney Weil, a local businessman, took over the team and engineered a number of good trades, bringing in outfielder Chick Hafey, third baseman Wally Gilbert, the flamboyant Babe Herman (from the equally hapless Dodgers) and, in 1931, slugger Ernie Lombardi.

Famous for his heroic nose and a running style that resembled an overweight cow plodding through a pasture, Lombardi became a fan favorite and one of baseball's great stars. He had broken in with the Pacific Coast League as an eighteen-year-old and hit .370 in three seasons there. He hit .297 for the Dodgers, who bought his contract, but for some unknown reason they traded him to Cincinnati. He was a durable catcher who caught one hundred games a year for ten straight seasons and topped .300 seven times. In 1938 Lombardi hit .342 and won the National League's MVP award.

CHAPTER FOUR

VICTORY AND VINDICATION

1934–1940

What really annoyed the bankers who owned the Reds was the knowledge that it was not the Depression that was keeping the fans away—it was the awful baseball played by their team. If people didn't have money, why did the Negro League teams who leased Redland Field and other ballparks in the city for their games consistently pull between ten and twenty thousand fans? The answer, of course, was good, hard baseball.

Black baseball had been a part of the Cincinnati landscape at least as far back as 1887. By the mid-1920s, Cincinnati had become such a good market for black baseball that when the Negro National League was formed it was picked for a franchise. The Cuban Stars, barnstormers for thirty-four years and an NNL team, moved from New York to Cincinnati in 1921, leasing Redland Field for their games. Later, in 1934, the Cincinnati Tigers came into the NNL (they, too, leased Redland) and remained in the league for three seasons. With an NNL team, Cincinnati fans, black and white, came in droves to see the great black stars of the 1920s and 1930s, legends like Satchel Paige, Josh Gibson, Cool Papa Bell, and Buck Leonard.

The bank, knowing that fans would turn out for good baseball, was determined first to find a solid, veteran baseball man to rebuild the ball

Do catchers have large hands? Ernie Lombardi holds seven baseballs in his right hand, with room for more, before a 1937 game. Lombardi, one of the most powerful hitting catchers in league history, hit .306 lifetime, with 190 home runs. In his years with the Reds, he caught over 100 games ten years in a row and hit over .300 in seven of those seasons. In 1938, he was MVP with a .342 average, nineteen homers and ninety-five RBIs. He was elected to the Hall of Fame in 1985.

61

club and sell tickets and second, down the road, to find a new owner with deeper pockets than Sidney Weil.

The first task brought them to the doorstep of Larry MacPhail, who had run several minor league clubs and spent a year with the Cardinals. Someone at the bank had the sense to hire MacPhail as general manager. He was an innovative genius who in Cincinnati and, later, in New York would not only build attendance and make champions of his teams, but revolu-

tionize baseball more than any man since Abner Doubleday.

MacPhail took over in the winter of 1934 and realized that, despite some February trades, there wasn't much he could do with his moribund team. What he needed were stars—soon to be stars, stars with a few years left in them. But stars cost money, and the team he had agreed to run was dead broke. In search of money, MacPhail wound up sitting in the office of Powel Crosley, Jr., a tall, thin, aris-

The first night game in the majors was at Crosley Field on May 24, 1935. Powel Crosley, here, threw the light switch in Cincinnati at the same time President Franklin Roosevelt, via wire, threw it in the White House, illuminating the totally dark ballpark and ushering in a new era for baseball. The Reds, pulling small crowds, were hoping night ball would attract people who worked all day. They were right. Night crowds for 1935 were more than double day crowds.

By 1934 the Reds were floundering. Powel Crosley, who made his fortune as an inventor of appliances and radios and owned a radio network, bought the team that spring. He became an innovator in baseball, authorizing the majors' first night game in 1935, hiring the first play-by-play radio broadcaster, and sponsoring hundreds of different promotions to sell tickets.

tocratic Cincinnati man who had made millions inventing cars, refrigerators, appliances, and radios. McPhail convinced Crosley that if he didn't step in, the team would be sold to interests in another city, and the Reds would be gone after sixty-five years of baseball.

Crosley agreed to buy the team, changing the name of the ballpark from Redland to Crosley Field, and he gave MacPhail carte blanche to beef up the lackluster ball club. McPhail did it, and not just by buying players. MacPhail was a showman who knew that what you tried to do was as important as what you actually did, and that the theater was as impressive as the show. He told Crosley the Reds had to spend money to make money. In the spring of 1934 he made a much-publicized attempt to buy Babe Ruth from the Yankees and install him as the Reds' player-manager (he failed). On June 8, 1934, MacPhail chartered two airplanes to fly his team from Cincinnati to Chicago for a weekend series of games. It was the first time any ball club flew from one city to another.

MacPhail's most extraordinary move, though, was one that changed baseball forever, with just the flip of a switch. He shared the complaints of all baseball executives that midweek attendance was cut down by sunset. Games started at three

Rain delay? In 1937, Cincinnati suffered some of the worst damage in its history when the Ohio River flooded. Crosley Field was under eight feet of water, which covered the entire field and swept up over most of the first deck of seats. These two Huck Finns are rounding second and headed for third.

The Cincinnati Tigers were a Negro League team that played in town from 1934 to 1937. The Tigers played other black teams and major league all-star teams in the off-season. In 1937 the team drew so many people to local parks that it had to rent Crosley Field to handle the crowds, which often approached 15,000.

Paul Derringer was one of the Reds' steadiest pitchers in the 1930s, winning twenty or more games three years in a row (1938–40) and, lifetime, had thirty-two shutouts. He won a high of twenty-five games in 1939. In 1940, Derringer won twenty and Buckey Walters twenty-two to lead the Reds to the world champi-onship. He was sold to the Cubs in 1943 and helped lead them to a pennant in 1945, winning sixteen games.

o'clock so they could end by five or six, but most people worked until five or six and could not get to day games. Attendance at Cincinnati midweek day games in 1934 was often just about a thousand. What baseball needed was night games and lights, MacPhail told Crosley. It was not a totally new concept. Back in 1915 the Tip Tops, the Federal League team in Brooklyn, went as far as preliminary wiring to put up lights at their ballpark but ran out of money. Night baseball became a reality in 1930, when the Negro League champions, the Kansas City Monarchs, developed a system of portable lights that were carried and raised on flatbed trucks. Their attendance more than tripled with lights. So, on May 24, 1935, the lights debuted at Crosley Field. Franklin D. Roosevelt himself flipped the switch at the White House, and a new era began.

Did it help? Well, that first night game drew 20,422 people, ten times the team's average attendance. It wasn't just the novelty, either: Night games that year routinely drew around twenty thousand fans; at one, an August 1 game against the rival Cardinals, nearly forty thousand jammed the field. Police had to seat the overflow crowd along the foul lines and in the outfield. In fact, thanks to lights, atten-dance in 1935 more than doubled that of 1934—topping 448,000.

The Cincinnati fan who kept his ticket stub from the 1938 All-Star Game, one of several played in Cincinnati over the years, did it for a good reason—the Reds Johnny Vander Meer won the game for the National League, 4–1.

Radio also emerged as a factor during the late 1930s. Radio needed baseball, and baseball, particularly the Reds, needed radio. A radio broadcast was free advertising, as were newspaper reports, but unlike the newspapers, the airwaves reached out across the Ohio River and up to Lake Erie and into Indiana and down into Kentucky and West Virginia. Radio extended for hundreds of miles and thousands upon thousands of people who knew little about the Reds began listening to them on the radio and became fans. Later, when the Reds became contenders, these fans would get to the ballpark and swell the box office.

"I heard my first Reds game on the radio in 1935," said fan Tom Downing, age 66, of Raceland, Kentucky. "I'll never forget it. A game coming to my little town all the way from Cincinnati? For a kid, that was just unbelievable. All the kids followed the Reds on radio throughout the area. The radio built the fan base that the team has had the last sixty years."

While Downing was tuning to the Reds in his town, others were doing the same in theirs. "You've got to remember that maybe the Reds were the only pro team in that whole Ohio, Indiana, West Virginia, and Kentucky area, but you had the black teams in the 1930s, hundreds, and I mean hundreds, of semi-pro teams.

That 1938 season was a tremendous one for the Reds, now managed by quiet "Deacon" Bill McKechnie. They waged a heated battle with three other teams for the pennant all year and even though they wound up fourth, they were just six games out of first. McCormick, the rookie, hit a stout .327 and had 209 hits. It was Ernie Lombardi's best year; he hit .342, winning the batting crown and MVP award. On the mound Paul Derringer won twenty-one games.

If you paid your quarter to ride the trolley on the Fourth of July, you could go to the Reds-Pirates doubleheader.

Every town had a team and every county had a league. You had a lot of baseball and all of that served as a real foundation for the majors and the Reds," said Paul Hall, of Foster, Kentucky, who started listening on radio in 1938.

If the radio developed the fans, MacPhail and his successor, mild-mannered Warren Giles, brought the players. The team was struggling through lackluster seasons in 1935, 1936, and 1937, but the key players were arriving. Slugger Babe Herman came in from Brooklyn in 1935. Kiki Cuyler was on board in 1936. Outfielder Ival "Goodie" Goodman, shortstop Billy Myers, and third baseman Lew Riggs were acquired. Rookie Frank McCormick arrived in the spring of 1938.

Manager Bill McKechnie graces the cover of this 1938 Reds score book. Note the price of bleacher tickets, just sixty cents.

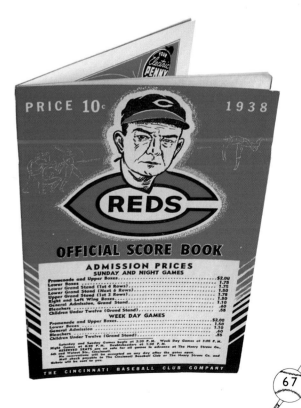

Pitcher Johnny Vander Meer (second from left) is hustled off field after hurling his second consecutive no-hitter in Brooklyn on June 15, 1938. The feat has never been equaled.

Everybody wanted Johnny Vander Meer's autograph when the Reds visited the Polo Grounds in New York on June 23, 1938. The Reds pitcher made history the week before, throwing two consecutive no-hitters.

You didn't show your face in Cincinnati in the fall and winter of 1939 if you weren't wearing one of these buttons.

The 1938 season, though, belonged to only one man—pitcher Johnny Vander Meer. After a lazy rookie year with a 3-5 record in 1937 he electrified the nation on June 11, when he tossed a no-hitter against Boston at Crosley Field. Vander Meer's next start was memorable. It was against the Dodgers in Brooklyn on June 15, and it was the Dodgers' first-ever night game (the Reds' old general manager, MacPhail, was head man in Brooklyn now and was doing for them what he had done for Cincinnati). Johnny had a fair first inning, a good second, a good third. As the night wore on it became wildly possible that the most historic thing about it would not be the lights. On that charmed warm summer night, Vander Meer put down everyone and threw another no-hitter, the only time a pitcher has hurled back-to-back no-hitters. "People forget that in my third start I went another three innings of no-hit ball. Hey, I was red hot that week. On fire. Nobody could touch me. I could have had three no-hitters, four. It was just a groove I got in that was perfect," said Vander Meer.

If 1938 was a good year for the Reds, 1939 was Shangri-La. That's the year they won it all, winning twelve straight in May on the way to a pennant that was not clinched until the very last series of the season, against the second-place Cardinals.

The Reds put a consistent lineup on the field every day in 1939. McCormick hit .332, Goodie Goodman .323, Lonny Frey .291, Billy Myers .381. Lombardi hit twenty homers. It was on the mound, though, that the Reds were invincible. Vander Meer was hurt most of the year, but Junior Thompson and Whitey Moore each won thirteen games, and Derringer won twenty-five. The real star was Bucky Walters, who brought with him to the mound an unusual history. Clean-shaven, clean-cut, smartly dressed Walters never wanted to pitch. He wanted to hit. He

NEWS *of the* **REDS**

Gabriel Paul, Editor   Lee Allen, Associate Editor
Vol. V.   Crosley Field — May 21, 1939   No. 4

CUBS HERE FOR TWO GAMES MEMORIAL DAY

Bucky Walters Flashes Championship Form

Morning Tilt at 10 A.M.; Second Contest at 3 P.M.

Bucky Walters

Dodgers Here Tomorrow, Tuesday

The Brooklyn Dodgers will appear here in single games tomorrow and Tuesday, with play starting at 3 P.M.

Home Schedule for Month

	May 22, 23
	May 24, 25
Brooklyn	May 29, 30
New York	(Two Games, A. M. & P. M.)
Chicago	June (14), 15 (Night Games)
Philadelphia	
• Sunday games	( ) Ladies' Day Games.

Bucky Walters had one of the strangest odysseys in the majors. Originally a pitcher, he was used at third base, first by the Braves and then the Red Sox in the early 1930s. The Phillies, who acquired him in 1934, let him pitch again but he was dreadful (11–21 in 1936). He went to Cincinnati in 1938, and when they gave him a chance to pitch, he put together two fine back-to-back seasons, posting a 27–11 record in 1939 and a 22–10 mark in 1940.

70

Who in the Queen City didn't want to belong to the Johnny Vander Meer fan club? Vander Meer, who stunned the sports world with back-to-back no-hitters in 1938, was one of the Reds' most popular players.

JOHNNY VANDER MEER FAN CLUB
845 Webster Street
Dayton, Ohio

MEMBERSHIP CARD

of *Howard Shough*

Johnny Vander Meer,
Honorary Pres.

Arlene Grillmeier,
Pres.

Howard Shough,
Vice-Pres.

Mildred Schell,
Secy.-Treas.

spent his early career as a third baseman. When he was sold to the Phillies in 1934, the coaching staff, saddled with one of the worst mound staffs in the majors, remembered that he had pitched a bit in the minors and made him a starting hurler. He didn't pitch well for Philadelphia, but he caught fire with the Reds in 1939, going 27-11, and confusing every batter in the league with his sidearm style and a darting fastball that left the mound low and then dropped sharply when it reached the plate. He baffled everybody, winning the MVP and leading the Reds to their first pennant in twenty years.

Cincinnati was thrilled over the pennant, the first since the ill-fated 1919 season. There were parades, parties, and speeches; everyone hoped the Reds could

right the wrong done them in the 1919 series. Unfortunately, Cincinnati's best Reds team in years was up against the invincible New York Yankees, who had stormed to their fourth straight American League pennant, taking it by seventeen games over an excellent Red Sox team, and were looking for their fourth straight World Series flag. They had Joe DiMaggio, Charlie "King Kong" Keller, Bill Dickey, and Joe Gordon in the lineup and Red Ruffing and Lefty Gomez on the mound. They were perhaps the strongest team in history.

All people remember about the series is that the Yankees swept it, four games to none, and took home their fourth straight world title. But it wasn't easy. Game one was a 2-1 squeaker for the Yanks, with Derringer baffling the Bombers

71

These tickets were to the third and fourth games of the 1939 World Series. The Yanks won the fourth and final game in the tenth inning following three errors by the Reds.

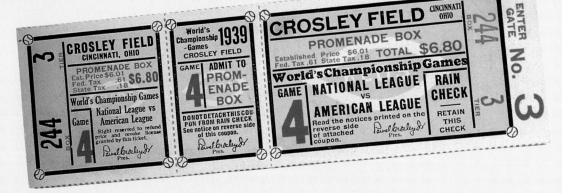

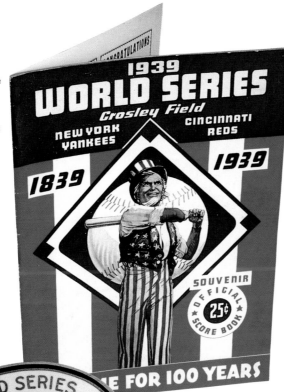

Uncle Sam graced the cover of this 1939 World Series program. Uncle Joe DiMaggio and his Yankees won it, though, four games to none.

Not many members of the press corps thought the Reds would take the 1939 World Series against the powerhouse Yankees. They were right. The Yankees swept the Reds in four games, even though big Frank McCormick hit .400.

with a vast array of pitches, only to lose. Monte Pearson threw a two-hitter in game two to nail down a 4-0 win for New York. Game three, in Cincinnati, went to New York by a 7-3 count. Game four went to the Yankees, 7-4, following a bizarre incident at the plate. Frankie Crosetti, on third, scored on DiMaggio's single to right. The Reds fielder bobbled the ball, and Keller, who was on second, steamed home and crashed into catcher Lombardi, who was dazed and dropped the ball. As Lombardi lay motionless, DiMaggio scored all the way from first, sliding under the finally roused catcher.

"It's ridiculous to say we had an easy time with the Reds, just ridiculous," said Lefty Gomez later. "It was a much closer series than it appeared on paper. Cincinnati played well."

Furious with the turn of events in October 1939 and looking for revenge, the Reds bolted out of the gate in April 1940 and raced to another pennant. Lombardi hit .319; McCormick had 191 hits and forty-four doubles and was league MVP. Walters won twenty-two and Derringer twenty. The Reds took over first in early July, survived the August suicide of backup catcher Willard Hershberger, and went on to take the flag.

This time the Yankees were not in the series for the first time in years.

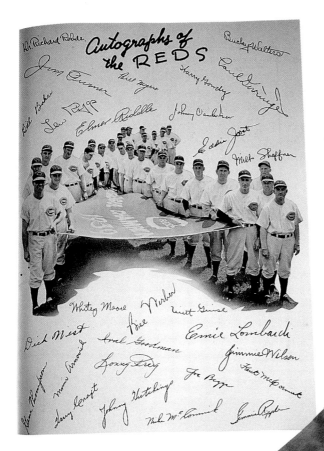

This page from a 1940 Reds yearbook contains facsimile autographs of the 1939 pennant winners.

Despite a valiant late-season drive, they lost the flag to Detroit by just two games. The Tigers were not lucky that year—they were good. Detroit had sluggers Hank Greenberg and Rudy York, shortstop Dick Bartell, catcher Birdie Tebbetts, and Hall of Famer Charlie Gehringer. Meanwhile, the Reds were hurting badly. Frey broke his toe in the last game of the season and was out of the series. Lombardi hurt his ankle and was out, too. With Hershberger gone the Reds had no catcher. The shaky solution was to reactivate Jimmie Wilson, a retired coach who had been a catcher. The out-of-shape Wilson strapped on the shin guards and crouched behind the plate.

The centennial patch graces this 1939 jersey of pitcher Al Hollingsworth, who never won more than twelve games in a season but somehow managed to hit a grand slam in 1936.

This pristine ticket stub from game six of the 1940 World Series was preserved inside a closed book for fifty years. The Reds won, 4-0, as Walters hit a home run to top off his shutout pitching.

Yes, they won it. The 1940 World Series was a squeaker, but the Reds held on to win game seven (2-1) and the series, four games to three. All of Cincinnati celebrated their first world championship since the tainted win in 1919.

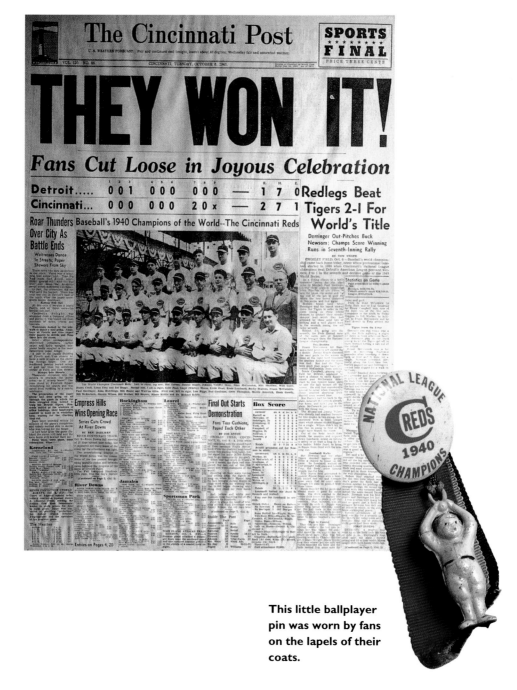

This little ballplayer pin was worn by fans on the lapels of their coats.

These mugs were among the many souvenirs sold after the 1940 series win.

The teams split the first two games and Detroit won the third, 7-4. Derringer came back with a win in game four to even the series. In game five Bobo Newsom, the flamboyant Tiger hurler, tossed a three-hitter, and Detroit hammered Cincinnati 8-0. Crucial game six was won by Bucky Walters two ways. He pitched a 4-0 shutout and in the eighth inning hit a home run.

Game seven was a thriller. Detroit held on to a one-run lead into the seventh, when McCormick scored on Jimmy Ripple's double to tie it up. And who should move Ripple to third and into scoring position? The old war-horse, Coach Jimmie Wilson. His sacrifice fly got Ripple to third, and then Ripple scored to move the Reds ahead 2-1. Derringer shut down the Tigers the rest of the way, and Cincinnati won its second, and its best, World Series. No asterisks, no controversies, no scandals, no bans, no fixes . . . just rings.

77

GEARING UP
1940s–1969

The rain came down heavy from the sky, like a bathtub plug had suddenly been pulled, drenching the banks of the Ohio River. It plunged from the heavens in sheets, hammering the roof of Crosley Field. In the stands, thousands of people bolted from their unprotected box and reserve seats and scampered toward the overhangs. The players ran into the dugouts. The men on the ground crew raced onto the field at a fast trot and began to unroll the heavy dark brown tarpaulin over the infield. Up above the mezzanine, in the press box, WKRC radio announcer Waite Hoyt shook his head gently from side to side and pushed his chair back ever so slightly from the counter in front of him, where the microphone was.

"Looks like a bit of a rain delay folks. That reminds me of the time. . . ."

Under the stands, people pulled out radios and tuned them to WKRC. Across Cincinnati, people listening to the game called friends who were not and gave them the good news: Rain delay. . . . Waite Hoyt is telling stories.

And he did on that summer night in 1954 as the showers continued to fall, just as he did during every rain delay. He would tell long, involved stories about his days as a pitcher with the Yankees, spin yarns about Babe Ruth's antics, the power of the old "Murderers Row" lineup of the

Waite Hoyt, a great pitcher for the New York Yankees who won 237 games in his career, became a Reds broadcaster in 1941 and remained at the mike through 1965. He became part of the fabric of Cincinnati sports and city life with his endless and fascinating stories about the game and its players.

79

CINCINNATI REDS' HOME GROUNDS

BROADCASTS ARE SPONSORED BY GENERAL MILLS "WHEATIES" • SOCONY VACUUM • MOBILGAS and MOBILOIL

LISTEN TO THE REDS GAMES ON WHIO 1290 ON YOUR DIAL • OUTSTANDING C.B.S. PROGRAMS

WHIO radio used a photo of Crosley to advertise its coverage of the games. The Reds pioneered the use of radio back in the 1930s.

By 1956 more than thirty radio stations broadcast Reds games, and millions of fans tuned in every night to listen to broadcaster Waite Hoyt.

1927 Yankees, tell tales of his classic matchups with Satchel Paige and the Homestead Grays on barnstorming trips, recount the card games he had seen, the parties he had been to. He was never the centerpiece of the story, either, just the teller of the tale. He would go on and on into the night, making vivid movies with his words, absolutely mesmerizing his audience until the rain stopped falling or the game was called.

By the early 1950s, radio dominated the media in the Ohio Valley areas within two hours of Crosley Field. It had begun to grow in the late 1930s but by the early

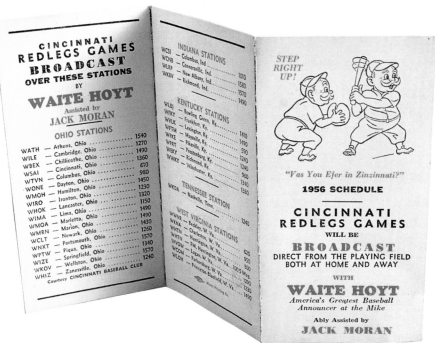

80

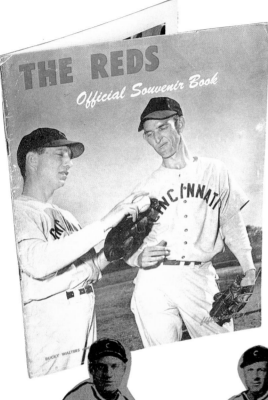

Pitching stars Bucky Walters, left, and Ewell Blackwell adorn the cover of this Reds souvenir book from the 1940s.

1950s, radio reigned. Attendance had dropped because the Reds struggled through each season, but the people who didn't go to the game listened on the radio and remained fans. Hoyt and WKRC also built a whole new fan base of kids, a base that would grow and bloom in the 1960s and 1970s.

Hoyt was a great pitcher for the Yankees, posting a 22-7 record in 1927 and anchoring one of baseball's best mound staffs. On retirement he did small pregame shows on New York radio and in 1942, to the surprise of all, won an audition as the new play-by-play man for WKRC (there were few ballplayers in broadcasting then).

Four-inch-high stand-up cards were popular in the 1940s.

Like most teams, the Reds had a Knot Hole Club that allowed thousands of kids to attend games on heavily discounted tickets.

"He was a show, a radio by himself. People who didn't even like baseball tuned him in. When it would rain, people would turn him on all over Ohio just to listen to those great stories of his," said John Dreyer, a fan who listened to Hoyt as a kid.

Fans loved the way he described games with a rich narrative full of anecdotes and color. "The game was more colorful on the radio than it was in the ballpark," said fan Dorothy Savaitch.

His finest hour was the night Ruth died. Word was passed to him during the game that his old friend, with whom he had closed many bars in New York, was gone. He announced it during the game and asked fans to stay tuned afterward because he planned to give a little eulogy. The eulogy was a two-hour discourse on the Babe, a one-man ramble filled with marvelous stories that went down as one of the great broadcasts in radio history.

A Reds ashtray from 1952.

This cardboard cutout character appeared in many bars and restaurants in the early 1950s.

burly slugger Ted Kluszewski, who came to the team in 1947 and had been launching baseballs over walls ever since. He hit twenty-five in 1950 and forty in 1954. He hammered forty-nine in 1954, forty-seven in 1955, and thirty-five in 1956. He hit over .300 in seven seasons.

"He was a huge guy, but I never realized how bulky and heavy he was until he stepped on my foot in a spring training game," said the Yankees' Gil McDougald. "It was like a building coming down on me."

Yankee pitcher Allie Reynolds still shakes his head when he talks about the 225-pounder. "He had amazing strength. His line drives were coming out at 150

Birdie Tebbets, nicknamed for his birdlike, high-pitched voice, managed the Reds in the 1950s.

miles per hour. I remember one day Big Klu hit three balls right back at me on the mound. I ducked on the first two and jumped up to avoid the third. When he got to first I yelled over at him 'Hey, Klu, from now on, hit them out at the outfielders, will you?'"

But what Kluszewski was most famous for were his huge arms. They changed history in more ways than one. When the slugger first came to the team he couldn't get his mammoth arms

85

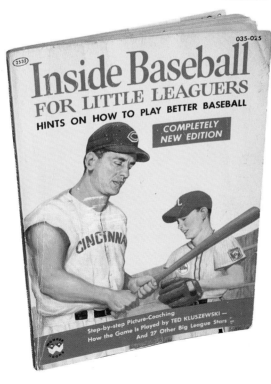

Home and away jerseys of Big Klu.

Who better than Klu, in his trademark sleeveless jersey, to teach little leaguers how to play ball?

through the sleeves of his jersey. The equipment manager got him bigger and bigger shirts, but he still couldn't fit. Finally, the frustrated Klu just took a pair of scissors and cut off both sleeves at the top and shoved his arms through. The sleeveless jersey made him look like Conan the Barbarian. The other players liked the sleeveless look and several more cut off their sleeves. The owners liked the look so much—the intimidating bare arms on warm days and the bright red undershirts covering the length of the arm on cold ones—that they just ordered all new, sleeveless uniforms. Fans from coast to coast loved the look.

They loved the rejuvenated Reds, too. In addition to Klu in 1954, the Reds had center fielder Gus Bell, who hit seventeen homers that year and went on to get 100 RBIs four different times, rookie Wally Post, who hit eighteen, and left fielder Jim Greengrass, who hit twenty-seven. Johnny Temple was at second and Roy McMillan at short. They also signed their first black player, Chuck Harmon, and the first player from Puerto Rico, Nino Escalera. These men formed the foundation of a team that finished between first and fifth in nine of the next ten years.

Post was a darling of the fans. He was a wild swinger who struck out as often as

Abe Stark's sign so often at Ebbets Field, in Brooklyn, that he became one of America's best-dressed men. Wally Post was a wonder at it. He hammered the suit sign above the left-field wall at Crosley eleven times. In the Reds sleek sleeveless uniforms and his tailored suits, he was the sharpest-looking man in Cincinnati on and off the field.

The success of the team showed at the box office, where attendance jumped

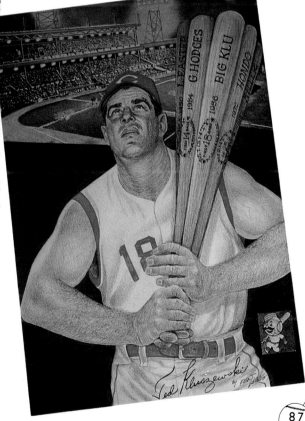

Big Ted Kluszewski couldn't get his gargantuan arms into the jerseys the trainers gave him and in frustration took a pair of scissors and cut the sleeves off.

he hit home runs. He hit forty home runs and had 109 RBIs in 1955. Post was legendary in one of baseball's most unusual categories, the hit-sign-win-suit league. In those days, just about every stadium had an outfield fence advertisement for a clothing store that would give a free suit to any player who hit it. It always attracted attention and built sales. Stan Musial hit

Wally Post's away jersey.

to 704,000 in 1954 and to 1.1 million in 1956 and 1957. "It was a great baseball team to watch, even if they didn't win a pennant. They played hard, they hit home runs, they made great catches. You couldn't ask for more in a ball club," said fan Wendell McCourt, who saw them in those years. "And, off the field, they were nice guys. You'd see them on the street and they'd stop and talk to you like they were a close friend."

The 1950s also saw the triumphant return of young Joe Nuxhall, who was signed at the age of fifteen in 1944, the youngest player ever. He pitched seven innings, was shelved, and wallowed in the

ally Post was never appreciated. Here was a guy who hit 210 home runs and once hit 40 in a season. He was one of the most powerful hitters I ever saw, and I saw all of them in my time. He'd hit homers over that left field fence at Crosley that were longer than Kluszewski's, yet he was never considered a star outside of Cincinnati. That was a shame.

—PAUL HALL, 76, OF FOSTER, KENTUCKY

Wally Post actually started as a pitcher in the minors, but his long ball hitting made him a regular in the outfield as soon as he got to the majors. He hit forty home runs in 1955 and thirty-six the next season (many over the left-field wall) and became one of the most popular Reds of the 1950s.

A Reds bumper sticker from 1957.

This megaphone was fashioned from a popcorn box. Fans finished their popcorn, punched out the bottom, and screamed at the umpire.

minors for seven years. He came back to the Reds and went 12-5 in 1954, 17-12 in 1955, and 13-11 in 1956 (he then went on to become the Reds announcer). He was joined on the mound by Art Fowler, Brooks Lawrence, and Johnny Klippstein.

By the time the 1956 season started, Cincinnati had all the players it needed to challenge for the pennant. A slender young rookie, an unheralded kid named Frank Robinson, wasn't even counted on for the pennant drive that spring. The team started winning in April and never stopped. It had many weapons—base stealers, good pitchers, double play combination, shrewd managing—but its howitzer was the home run. The Reds crushed baseballs that summer. Someone said they must have a spe-

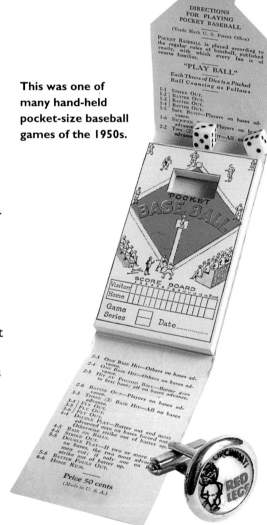

This Reds charm bracelet was among the numerous souvenirs produced in the 1950s.

cial factory in Haiti just to make the balls the Reds knocked into neighborhoods.

The Reds sluggers hit 221 homers (a record broken by the 1961 Yankees with 240). They hit eight in one game against Milwaukee and forty-four against the Dodgers for the season. Klu's season total was thirty-five, Post's was thirty-six, and Bell's twenty-nine. Even little-known catcher Ed Bailey socked twenty-eight. And the rookie, Robinson? Well, he stunned baseball that year. He not only hit thirty-eight home runs, but he had eighty-three RBIs and a .290 average, winning Rookie of the Year honors to start one of baseball's most fabulous careers.

The hard-hitting lineup kept the Reds in first much of the year, but Cincinnati hearts were broken in the end when they finished just two games in back of the Dodgers.

There was nothing wrong with the hitting in 1957. Frank Robinson hit .322 with twenty-nine home runs in 1957 and

This was one of many hand-held pocket-size baseball games of the 1950s.

What true fan would be caught dead at a fancy dinner without his 1950s Redlegs cuff links and tie clasp.

This was Joe Nuxhall at age fifteen, just before he reported to the Reds in 1944. He bombed in his first outing and was dispatched to the minors, but returned seven years later to compile a 135–117 record.

Joe Nuxhall was the youngest pitcher to hurl in the majors in the twentieth century, pitching a single inning at the end of the 1944 season at age fifteen. He later became a popular Reds broadcaster.

hit twenty-five more in 1958 and thirty-one in 1959. George Crowe hit thirty-one homers, Gus Bell hit .292, and Don Hoak .293. But Kluszewski missed half of 1957 with an injury and was traded. The pitching staff went on siesta (only two hurlers had winning records). The bullpen was weak. And those hard, cynical Cincinnati fans? They stayed unbelievably loyal. Loyal? Not only did more than a million of them turn out at Crosley for the undistinguished season, but they stuffed the All-Star ballot

CINCINNATI REDS' PITCHER JOE NUXHALL

boxes and managed to vote eight Reds into the National League lineup. The rigged voting was such a travesty that Commissioner Ford Frick tossed three of the "elected" players off the team.

The 1958 season was worse as the Reds were fourth again. Tebbetts, disgruntled, quit; Jimmy Dykes took over. Unnoticed, the Reds brought up hot-hitting rookie outfielder Vada Pinson and pitcher Jim O'Toole. By 1960, when Fred Hutchinson took over as manager, shortstop Leo "Chico" Cardenas had been added, along with pitchers Joey Jay and Jim

tries). Gordy Coleman hit .287 with twenty-six home runs, Gene Freese hit 26 homers, and Wally Post hit .294 with twenty homers while playing just half the season. Chico Cardenas, also playing part time, hit .308. Jerry Lynch came out of nowhere to hit .315 in ninety-six games and hit .404 as a pinch hitter. A delightful surprise was Vada Pinson, who hit .343. But it was the pitching that carried the Reds into the World Series. Jay was 21-10,

A perky Bob Purkey graces one of the silly money bills sold to fans in 1961.

Brosnan, catcher Johnny Edwards, and first baseman Gordy Coleman. Quietly, the Reds front office had built a winner—it just wasn't winning yet.

All of that changed in 1961, just a few months after the death of Powel Crosley. The Reds, with superior pitching, battled the Dodgers for the pennant all summer. In mid-August, O'Toole and Bob Purkey hurled back-to-back shutouts against the Dodgers, derailing them.

Everything worked for the Reds that year. The lineup was one of the most productive in Reds history. Robinson, who was by then one of the best players in the game, won the MVP award with his thirty-seven home runs, 124 RBIs, .323 average, and 22 stolen bases (in just twenty-five

Gordy Coleman was a football player turned baseball star. He came up in the early 1960s and hit 28 homers to help lead the Reds to the 1961 pennant.

Reds souvenir playing cards from 1961.

Cincinnati had many aces on its mound staff in 1961 and a few more in this souvenir pack of playing cards.

A high school star out of the same school that produced Frank Robinson and Curt Flood, Vada Pinson tore up the Pacific Coast and California leagues, hitting .357 in 1957–58 seasons. Called up in 1959, for the next ten years he was one of the mainstays of the Reds offense, hitting .286 lifetime with 256 home runs.

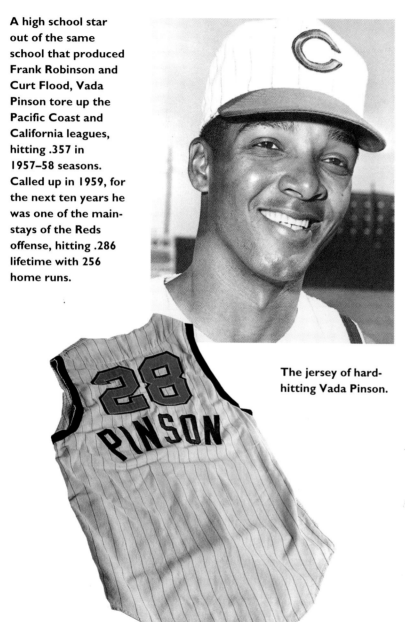

The jersey of hard-hitting Vada Pinson.

O'Toole 19-9, Purkey 16-12, and Brosnan 10-4. Brosnan even wrote a book about the Cinderella season, *Pennant Race,* to go with his other tome, *The Long Season.* Everybody who walked to the mound was a stopper.

"We had a team of great balance in '61," said Gordy Coleman. "Look at the lineup! You had three .300 hitters. . . . Jerry Lynch, the pinch hitter, hit .315. Whoever heard of a pinch hitter up as much as Jerry [181 at-bats] hitting .315? Great balance. If one guy didn't get a hit or drive in a run, another would. The pitching was solid. In O'Toole, Jay, Purkey, and Brosnan we had a superior mound staff. That team was tremendous."

Reds fans packed Crosley that year, and euphoria spread throughout the city when the pennant was won in the last week of September. There were parties, parades, special appearances by players on every television and radio show, tributes, dinners, and dances. There was an impending sense of doom in the air the week after, though, when fans realized the Reds had to meet one of the greatest Yankee teams of all time in the World Series.

The 1961 Yankees were the team that broke the Reds' home run record, with 240. Roger Maris broke Ruth's record with his sixty-one, Mantle hit fifty-four, and Moose Skowron twenty-eight. The three

The 1961 Reds may have been one of the best baseball teams of all time, but they ran into one of the very best, the New York Yankees, in the World Series and lost, four games to one.

Yankee catchers combined to hit sixty-four. Six New York pitchers had winning records. Whitey Ford won twenty-five games.

The Yanks jumped off to the lead as Ford pitched a 2-0 shutout, but Jay won game two to even the series. The championship moved to Crosley then, and with

the fans roaring, the Reds held a 2-1 lead going into the eighth. All things seemed possible. The Yanks, who lived and died by the home run, went to it again, though. Johnny Blanchard hit one out in the eighth to tie the game and Maris won the game with another homer in the ninth. That seemed to cripple the Reds. Ford came

Cincinnati Baseball Club
Copyright 1961

The *Cincinnati Enquirer* sold a *lot* of these newspapers. Euphoria died quickly in the series, though, as Whitey Ford shattered Babe Ruth's consecutive-scoreless-innings streak, and the Yanks won, four games to one.

THE CINCINNATI ENQUIRER

121st YEAR NO. 171—DAILY   WEDNESDAY MORNING, SEPTEMBER 27, 1961   FINAL EDITION—PRICE 7 CENTS

REDS WIN THE PENNANT

Victory Plus Dodger Loss Sews It Up

Crowds Jam Fountain Square To Ride The Reds Home

Pennant's Ours, Thousands Cry

Frenzied Red Fans Jam Fountain Square

back in game four and threw another shutout, 7-0, breaking Babe Ruth's all-time series consecutive-scoreless-innings record (Whitey had thirty-two). In the final, game five, the Yanks unloaded on Jay for five runs in the first and went on to a lopsided 13-5 win.

"Any other team, any other year, and we might have had a world championship," said Coleman. "Nobody could beat the Yankees that year."

The Yanks who played in that series agree. Said Mickey Mantle, years later: "The Reds were a good team. Good pitching, great hitting. The '61 Yankees were the best baseball team of all time, though, even better than the '39 Yankees or '27 Yankees with Ruth and Gehrig, and nobody was

Fans sported the pins, but the awesome 1961 Yankees, with Mantle and Maris, sported the rings after the World Series.

A fan kept this stub for his seat in the "sun deck." There was little sunshine as the Reds fell to the Yanks 13-5 that day, even with Mantle and Berra out of the New York lineup with injuries.

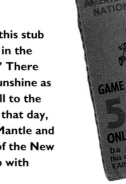

The *Cincinnati Post* put out a special issue to ballyhoo the 1962 Reds, who would be (unsuccessfully) defending their National League pennant.

going to even come close to us. Not the Reds, the Dodgers, the Giants. Nobody."

Even though they lost, the Reds were treated like heroes in the Queen City. They had won a pennant no one really expected and had given the town a summer to remember.

First baseman Gordy Coleman's National League championship ring from 1961.

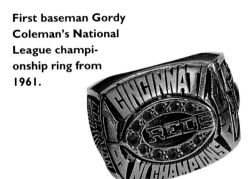

The 1961 season would prove to be the last chance for this generation of Reds. Frank Robinson had another sensational year in 1962, with a .342 average, thirty-nine homers, and 136 RBIs. Pinson had 100 RBIs, and Coleman hit twenty-eight homers. Purkey won twenty-three games; Jay twenty-one. Joe Nuxhall, traded away in 1960, was brought back at the end of the season and went 5-0. Nothing they did, even taking 98 games, helped them win the pennant, though, because that was the year both the Giants and the Dodgers won 101 games. The Reds slumped to fifth in 1963, as they traded an aging Wally Post early in the year.

But as the hero of one generation departed, that of a new generation arrived, in the form of the new second baseman, a local kid named Pete Rose. He hit .273 and was Rookie of the Year. "Nobody expected anything from him, and at the start of the season nobody but me asked him for

It's rare for any collector to own a complete uniform, socks and all, but one lucky fan managed to snare this one, which belonged to Billy McCool. One of the team's top relief pitchers in the 1960s, McCool had twenty-one saves in 1965 and eighteen in 1966.

You can almost see the tear stains on these phantom tickets to the 1964 World Series at Crosley that never was. The Reds management, certain the team would win the pennant, had thousands of them printed up, only to watch in disbelief as the Reds lost the flag to St. Louis on the final day of the season.

his autograph," said longtime fan Willie DeLuca. "I loved the way he hustled, how he'd slide head first all the time. I thought he was going to be good. I'd wait outside the locker room as the players went off the field and he'd always stop to sign something for me. Always. The other kids thought I was crazy, waiting for an unknown rookie, but I knew there was something about him."

In 1964 the Reds almost backed into a pennant. They were playing well in August and September but not making much progress when the Phillies suddenly collapsed. It enabled the Reds to surge forward, but they lost first place on the final day of the season to St. Louis.

This autographed bat is one of many Frank Robinson used to hit 334 home runs in Cincinnati before Bill DeWitt traded him away in the number-one blockhead trade in sports history. Robby, of course, went on to win the triple crown for Baltimore the next season.

33⅓ RPM

This LP, full of interviews and batting tips, was only one of many Reds records of Frank Robinson. He would set even more with the Orioles.

Some fans believe you should get down on one knee before a jersey of the immortal Frank Robinson. Fans were crushed when the front office traded him away to Baltimore.

99

Slugger Frank Robinson at bat in spring training in Tampa, Florida, in 1963. Robinson, a surprise home run hitter for the Reds, who didn't think much of him when he came up, was one of the most feared hitters in baseball.

This was one of many pieces of memorabilia sold in 1969.

The 1964 season was a sad one, though. Ailing manager Hutchinson, stricken with cancer, somehow got through the year with painkillers and then, when it was over, died. It was a personal loss, but a professional one, too. Without the capable Hutch, the team slipped badly, finishing no higher than third for the rest of the 1960s. Then, in 1965, Bill DeWitt, the new general manager, stunned Cincinnati and all of baseball when he traded superstar Frank Robinson to the Baltimore Orioles.

Bottom left, the Reds were expelled from the National League for selling beer at games in 1880. But in 1969 beer was still a part of the Cincinnati ballgame experience.

Center, the First National Bank of Cincinnati sponsored thousands of 1967 Reds schedules and handed them out all over town.

DeWitt said Robinson had reached his peak; he would start to go downhill and had to be unloaded. Over-the-hill Robinson went on to win the triple crown with the Orioles that next season (leading the league in batting average, homers, and RBIs) and would average thirty homers a year in his six seasons there. Fans and sportswriters proclaimed it the worst trade in baseball history.

Maybe it was. Ruth was in his very first season in 1914 when the Reds elected not to sign him. No one knew how good he would be. Frank Robinson? Everybody knew how good he was. This was like the

ten-year-old who trades away his mother's ten-thousand-dollar necklace to the kid next door for his bike.

The trade of Robinson in the middle of the decade coincided with the retirement of the beloved Waite Hoyt from the broadcast booth. Their departures marked an end to an era. Most of the top players from the 1961 team were gone, and the Reds were in decline. The old guard was passing, but others were arriving—people like Rose, Tony Perez, Johnny Bench—and when the 1970s dawned they would play baseball like few teams in the history of the game.

The 1968 yearbook was slick. The Reds were not, finishing fourth that season.

101

CHAPTER SIX

FULL THROTTLE
1970–1979

Everyone was working overtime in the spring of 1970 so that Riverfront Stadium, which would replace fading Crosley Field, would be ready to open for the major league All-Star Game in July. Riverfront was the jewel in Cincinnati's crown. Local businesspeople, the tourist industry, and the city council were counting on Riverfront, on the banks of the Ohio, to anchor a massive downtown revival that would turn both Cincinnati and its neighbor across the water, Covington, Kentucky, into bustling urban centers once again. Cincinnati's business district, like that of so many cities in the late 1960s, was in decay, and everyone, it seemed, was fleeing to suburbia. The city fathers were certain a brand new stadium, and the hype and prestige of the All-Star Game, would turn the fortunes of the Queen City around.

Construction crews worked overtime to complete baseball's largest parking garage, tucked nicely under the stadium. Grounds crews worked overtime to knit the artificial turf field into the ballpark. The Convention and Visitors Bureau worked overtime promoting the new stadium and, with it, the "new Cincinnati." But none of them, not in double overtime, weekends, or holidays, worked as hard as the Cincinnati Reds.

Fired up by their new manager, George "Sparky" Anderson, the team that finished third in the division in 1969, the first year of divisional

Sparky Anderson and Johnny Bench got ready to open yet another bottle of the bubbly to celebrate the Reds' dramatic 4–3 win in the seventh game of the 1975 Series, which writers claimed was the greatest of all.

103

Wherever he goes, Sparky Anderson wins pennants. He won with Detroit, but his great years were with Cincinnati. Here, Sparky, who won five divisional titles, four pennants, and two World Series, chats with Dave Concepcion.

104

play, roared out of the starting gate in 1970 at Crosley Field and leaped into first place, winning fifty of its first seventy games. The team hit 191 home runs, batted .270, and had a slugging average of .436. Johnny Bench hit forty-five homers; Tony Perez, forty; and Lee May, thirty-four. Hustling Bobby Tolan hit .316, and rookie Bernie Carbo hit .310. Pete Rose, by now a superstar, bat .316, with 205 hits, and added to his reputation as "Charlie Hustle" when he brutally mowed down catcher Ray Fosse to score the winning run in the bottom of the twelfth inning at the All-Star Game at Riverfront.

During the season a player, no one is quite sure who, called the club "the Big Red Machine," and the catchy nickname stuck. Like a powerful locomotive, the Reds would run over baseball teams for an entire decade.

The Reds won 102 games in 1970, took the divisional title by fourteen games, and then beat Pittsburgh for the pennant. The Machine ran out of gas in the World Series against the Orioles, though, as Baltimore third baseman Brooks Robinson put on one of the most dazzling displays of fielding in baseball history. The Orioles beat the Reds, four games to one, but the Reds returned home to an airport packed with thousands of cheering fans who knew 1970 was the start of something big.

Tony Perez, one of
the finest sluggers in
Reds history, retired
as the number 14
RBI leader in major
league history.
Perez, a third base-
man, came to the
Reds in 1964 and
drove in over 100
RBIs six times
between 1967 and
1976, piling up 1,652
lifetime.

Good old "Mr. Reds"
graced this and many
other flags in the
1970s (he used to
have a mustache).

1970s WORLD SERIES

Reds fans were inundated with an avalanche of souvenirs after the rousing 1975 World Series. True collectors have kept Reds Pepsi bottles, unopened, all these years.

Hope no one in Boston received one of these special Christmas cards— the Reds beat the Red Sox in the memorable 1975 World Series.

There was no way we were going to beat Baltimore [in 1970], because of Brooks Robinson. He was a human shovel at third— stopped everything. If Perez had hit a grand slam home run in game five, Robinson would have run to the outfield wall and jumped up to catch it.

—JOE DERMODY, 71, OF MILFORD, OHIO

I never got to a World Series when I was a kid, so when my grandson was eight, in 1970, I told him that if the Reds ever got into a series again I'd take him. Wouldn't you know it, six months later we were sitting in Riverfront for the World Series.

—LLOYD PETERSON, 70, OF CINCINNATI

A stub from the 1975 series, the greatest in history, some say.

Pete Rose signed this ticket stub from the sixth game of the 1972 World Series. The Reds won this one, 8-1, but lost the seventh and deciding game.

This mug was one of many pieces of memorabilia produced after the fabulous 1975 series win.

If any picture defined Peter Rose, "Charlie Hustle," it's this one. He's sliding face first into home, beating the tag of Giants catcher Dave Rader on July 30, 1972. Pete did make a lot of money in baseball, but so did his dry cleaner.

My hometown was Oakland, California, where Frank Robinson and Joe Morgan lived. Morgan was my mom's favorite player. Everybody in the neighborhood followed the Reds. On the high-school baseball team, they started an award called "Mr. Hustle," named after Pete Rose. I won that award. I still have it. So there was no doubt in my mind where I wanted to play baseball—Cincinnati, Ohio.

—BIP ROBERTS

"Let me tell you how good the Reds were in '70," said Ron Santo, of the Cubs. "The Orioles were far and away the best team in baseball in '69 but lost to the Miracle Mets in the series. In '70, the Orioles were better than they were in '69, if that's possible. They won 108 games that year! In baseball, that's like never losing."

The Reds slipped in 1971, finishing fourth as injuries riddled the lineup and Bench had an off year. In the middle of the summer, though, the Reds managed to that you'd win then. You never walked off the mound feeling bad," said Don Gullett.

The Reds beat the Pirate team of Willie Stargell and Roberto Clemente for the pennant in a heart-stopping, five-game play-off. The teams split the first two games. Pittsburgh won game three by a single run. The Reds won game four on a two-hitter pitched by Ross Grimsley. In the final game, a Bench home run in the ninth tied the score, and then smart running by George Foster put him in position to score the winning run on a wild pitch in the bottom of the ninth.

In the 1972 World Series, the Reds lost to the Oakland A's, one of the strongest teams in American League history, even without superstar Reggie Jackson, who had been injured in the play-offs. The A's had excellent pitching, with Catfish

Most people seem to think authors write only about the Yankees and Dodgers. This is a nice collection of books about the Reds, led by pitcher Jim Brosnan's excellent work *The Long Season*.

Jack Gilligan Says
"GO BIG RED MACHINE"

JOHNNY BENCH   JACK GILLIGAN   PETE ROSE

Broadcaster Jack Gilligan was featured in this two-and-a-half-by-three-inch promo card.

This was one of many posters marking the Reds' second straight mauling of the American League in the World Series of 1976.

Hunter, Blue Moon Odom, Vida Blue, Ken Holtzman, and reliever Rollie Fingers. It was a hard-played and extremely close World Series; six of the seven games were decided by one run, and no pitcher hurled a complete game. The A's took home the trophy on a slender 3-2 win in the seventh game.

The Reds again won the division crown in 1973, with Rose enjoying an MVP season—230 hits and a .338 average. Perez had twenty-seven homers, Morgan twenty-six, and Bench twenty-five. A late addition, Ken Griffey, hit .384. The play-offs against the Mets were marred by a fistfight between Rose and the Mets' shortstop

Bud Harrelson after a roughhouse slide into second by Rose. The game was halted the next inning when Rose was bombarded with debris by the fans. When it resumed, the Mets won. There was no October trip in 1974, either, as the Reds finished second to the Dodgers, even though they won ninety-eight games.

The 1975 and 1976 Reds teams were among the best in baseball, going as far back as when Albert Spalding was pitching for the Cubs in 1876. Everything clicked for the Big Red Machine those two years. Foster emerged as one of the top power

THE BIGGEST RED MACHINE

JOHNNY BENCH

I was a catcher on my school's softball team and I just adored Johnny Bench. To me, he was the greatest ballplayer that ever lived. The catcher never lived who could combine that power hitting with superb fielding, not Berra, not Campanella. Nobody.

—DOREEN SHELL, 36, OF INDIANAPOLIS

Johnny Bench gave out these caps to help promote his local television show.

A set of Bench equipment, plus his glove and bat. His gear was custom-made to fit his oversize legs and arms.

He was a pure slugger. When he was at bat you always moved back. He was a good hitter, but a clutch hitter. If there was one person in the American League or National League you'd want in there with people on in the ninth, it was Johnny.

—CARL YASTRZEMSKI, BOSTON RED SOX

Johnny Bench gave this warm-up jacket to a fan after the 1972 season.

He had big, strong hands, huge hands. His hands were bigger than people's thighs. It gave him the edge.

—YOGI BERRA

eople forget that during the decade of the Big Red Machine the Mets had good teams, the Dodgers had good teams, the Giants had good teams and the Cards had good teams. Some of the best players in baseball history played against the Reds in the Big Red Machine era. So what they did was no freak accident, it was sensational, historic baseball.

—GORDY COLEMAN,
FORMER REDS PLAYER AND ANNOUNCER

whole life and the next year he was terrific. He was the core of the team," said announcer Marty Brennaman.

Tony Perez nods in agreement. "Everybody knows what a good hitter he was, but people forget what a great defensive catcher he was. He caught one hundred games thirteen years in a row. That's some endurance for anybody."

Perez, too, was one of the cogs of the Big Red Machine in the 1970s. A first baseman who was converted into a third baseman, Perez hit .279 lifetime with 389 home runs. He had more than one hun-

dred RBIs six times in the 1970s, and always drove in runners on base. He finished his career fourteenth on the all-time RBI list with 1,652. Teammate Pete Rose shakes his head when talking about him. "Consistency. That was Tony. Year in, year out he knocked people in. He was big, strong and rarely struck out. He was always hitting .270 or .280 with thirty or so home runs. He'd hit lots of doubles. I'll tell you how consistent he was. When I saw a guy on [base] and him up, I'd know that guy would score."

Joe Morgan won back-to-back MVP awards in 1975 and 1976, a rare occurrence, and it capped a great career for him. Morgan, third in career walks, hit .271 lifetime, with 268 home runs and 1,134 RBIs in his long, twenty-one-year career. The slight, five-foot-seven-inch, 150-pound slugger had sensational seasons in 1975 and 1976. In 1975 he was not only league MVP but MVP in the All-Star Game. He hit .327 that year, with ninety-four RBIs and

This is the bat Joe Morgan used to knock in Ken Griffey for the winning run in the last inning of the last game in the heart-stopping 1975 series at Fenway Park.

If Joe Morgan the broadcaster interviewed Joe Morgan the player back in the 1970s, he'd ask, "How'd you do all that?" Morgan, just five-foot-seven and 150 pounds, had hit only about .260 in Houston before he arrived in Cincinnati in 1972. There he caught fire, hitting .292 that year and winning back-to-back MVP awards in 1975 and 1976. Good things do come in small packages.

These cards of Ken Griffey and George Foster celebrated the Reds' 1975 World Championship.

I was a kid in the 1970s and the Big Red Machine *was* baseball. As a kid, I just wanted to play here, where Rose and Foster and Morgan and those guys played.

—DARNELL COLES

Ironically, he was the three-thousandth strikeout victim for both Bob Gibson and Nolan Ryan ("I was just in the right place at the right time," he laughed).

The players of the Big Red Machine years think they know why the teams were so good. "People always tell me that the hardest thing in the world is for any ball club to stay on top for ten or twelve years. They're right. The Reds had a tremendous balance that made the team a winner. We never relied on one guy, or two guys, or three guys, to carry us. If your 3-4-5 hitters went 0-12 one night, we could still win the ball games because everybody else was good and played well. It was a well balanced team and a team that played together as a unit and, here's the hard part, did it year after year after year," said Bench.

"Heart," said Rose. "Everybody on that team had heart. They wanted to win the ball games every single time we stepped on the field."

In 1976, the Reds went on a barn-storming tour through Japan. This is a ticket stub from one of the games, plus an unusual Japanese Reds pin.

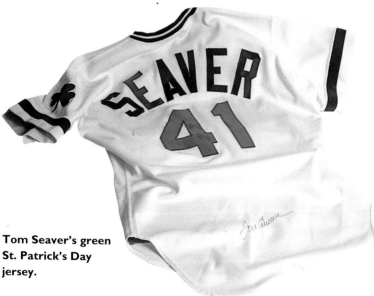

Tom Seaver's green
St. Patrick's Day
jersey.

120

The pitching for the Reds in the 1970s was not great, but Billingham, Nolan, Pat Zachry, and later Tom Seaver, Mike LaCoss, and Mario Soto could always be counted on to win fourteen or fifteen games a year. Without a single twenty-game winner, the 1975 mound staff nonetheless had the ability to consistently win ball games, which helped the Reds enormously that year. After a slow start, the Big Red Machine went into overdrive in June and July and then roared to 108 wins. They took the division by twenty games over a good Dodger team and then drubbed the Pirates in three straight for the pennant. The Machine was on a roll going into the 1975 series, a series that would be remembered as long as the game is played.

In October 1975 the Boston Red Sox came into the World Series after an upset win over the powerful Oakland A's in the league championship. The Sox had yet another chance to grab the brass World Series ring. They had made it to the series in 1946 and 1967 and lost. They had made it into the only two tie-breaking play-off games in American League history, in 1948 and 1978, and lost both of those, too. In fact the Red Sox had not won a World Series since 1918. In 1975 they were hungry and they were loaded. The team included outfielders Fred Lynn, Carl

As happens so often, an unresolved salary squabble sent Tom Seaver to the Reds in 1977. Unable to come to terms with the Hall of Fame pitcher, the Mets traded Seaver to Cincinnati in mid-season. Tom Terrific did not miss a step, finishing up a brilliant 21–6 season in Ohio. The next year, he threw a no hitter for the Reds, beating the Cards. He was 16–6 in 1979 with five shut outs. In the strike-shortened 1981 season, Seaver was near perfect with a 14–2 record. He was dealt back to the Mets in 1982.

Yastrzemski, and Dwight Evans; Carlton Fisk behind the plate; and solid hitters Rick Burleson and Rico Petrocelli. On the mound they had Bill Lee, Rick Wise, and Luis Tiant.

Boston, at home, took game one on a 6-0 shutout. The Reds managed to win game two by a single run, 3-2, in the ninth. The series moved to Riverfront Stadium and the Reds eked out a slender 3-2 win in ten innings in game three. The pendulum swung back to the Sox in game four as Tiant beat the Reds 5-4. Perez exploded with two homers and four RBIs in game five to lead an attack that staked Don Gullett to a 6-2 victory.

Then came game six in Boston. The lead seesawed back and forth until Foster's double in the seventh put the Reds up 5-3. A Geronimo homer in the top of the eighth stretched the lead to 6-3, and Cincinnati was suddenly six outs away from the championship. But in the bottom of the eighth, with two out, pinch hitter Bernie Carbo, who had come up with the Reds, belted a three-run homer to tie the game and send all of Boston into a frenzy. The score held through the ninth, tenth, and eleventh innings, and into the fateful twelfth. Fisk hit a towering fly ball that started out fair and began to hook ominously foul. Standing at the plate Fisk thrust both hands in the air and waved

again and again for the ball to stay fair. At the last moment, its hook straightened—it hit the foul pole for the game-winning home run. Boston was delirious.

The Red Sox had the momentum, and they had the home field advantage (which meant a lot in the tiny bandbox of Fenway), but Cincinnati would not say die. In the seventh game, down 3-0, the Reds tied it 3-3 with help from yet another home-run blast from Perez and won it, appropriately for such a close series, in the ninth, with Morgan singling to center to drive in Griffey. Cincinnati had its first world championship since 1940.

"It was a shame there couldn't be co-winners in that series because both teams played so well," said Bench.

Yastrzemski agreed. "It was like we were all part of something different, something very special, and, inning by inning, we all knew it," he said.

Just to make sure people knew the Big Red Machine hadn't lost a wheel in that historic World Series, the Reds romped through the National League in 1976, winning 102 games. Incredibly, the club led the league in homers, triples, doubles, runs, RBIs, team batting average, slugging, stolen bases, and bases on balls. The team also had the highest fielding percentage and made the fewest errors. The batting average, .280, was the highest the club had

Cesar Geronimo slides into third in the 1976 World Series, which the Reds won in a four game sweep of the Yankees.

scored in forty-six years. Rose again led the club in hits with 215, scored the most runs, 130, and hit the most doubles, forty-two. Foster hit 121 RBIs. Griffey hit .336 and lost the batting crown on the final day of the season. Morgan led in slugging with a .576 average and was MVP again. Seven pitchers won more than ten games.

The Big Red Machine rolled over Philadelphia in three straight to take the pennant and then had to tangle with a fierce New York Yankee team. The Bronx Bombers crushed everyone in their division that summer, finishing first by ten and a half games, and then beat Kansas City, three games to two, to take the pennant. The team featured Chris Chambliss (.293),

Graig Nettles (32 homers), Mickey Rivers (.312), and Thurman Munson (.302) in the lineup. On the mound, the Yanks had Catfish Hunter (seventeen wins), Ed Figueroa (nineteen wins), and Doc Ellis (seventeen wins). Sparky Lyle had twenty-three saves. As good as they were, the Yanks were mowed down in four straight. Naturally, the fourth and final game was won by Bench, who hit two home runs and drove in five runs. The Reds were the first team in the National League to win back-to-back world titles since the 1921-22 New York Giants under John McGraw.

The Machine needed oil in 1977. The front office foolishly traded Perez. Then Gullett became a free agent and left. The disheartened Reds were second despite Foster's fifty-two homers and Bench's thirty-one, and fine seasons from Griffey and Rose, who connected for two-hundred hits for the ninth year in a row. The Reds were second in 1978 despite Rose's historic forty-four-game hitting streak. In 1979, Rose was traded and, for no apparent reason, Anderson was fired, but the Reds, riding the arm of newly arrived Tom Seaver (16-6 with a no-hitter), still managed to win a divisional title, but lost the pennant to the Pirates.

Throughout the 1970s, the Reds participated in a fierce rivalry with the Los Angeles Dodgers just about every year to be the king of the Western Division.

Never in history have two teams in the same division been so good for a solid decade. Fighting for division supremacy made both better and turned their annual flag runs into a heated rivalry. Sparky Anderson's boys won four pennants and three world championships in the 1970s, but so did Walter Alston and Tommy Lasorda's boys. The Dodgers won world titles in 1974, 1977, and 1978, but also finished second to the Reds in 1970, 1972, 1975, and 1976.

"The Dodgers have rivalries with a number of teams, the Giants and Cards being the most talked about, but if you look at the records, you won't find a tougher rivalry than the Dodgers and Reds in the 1970s," said Lasorda. "Those guys were *good*."

When the 1970s ended the Big Red Machine had, in just ten years, won six divisional titles (they finished second three times), four pennants, and two (back-to-back) World Series. Three starters on those teams—Bench, Morgan, and Seaver—have been elected to the Hall of Fame, and three other members, Rose, Perez, and manager Anderson, probably will be. Along with the Yankees of the 1930s and 1950s and the turn-of-the-century Chicago Cubs, the Big Red Machine was among the greatest teams in baseball history.

Pete Rose's suitcase.

123

THE NEW REDS
1980s AND BEYOND

In June 12 in the middle of the 1981 season, unable to reach an agreement on a new contract system, the major league players went on strike. It was to last through August 9. America's ballparks were as vacant as ghost towns. Television networks broadcast old games. Newspapers reprinted game stories from battles of years gone by. The strike would cost the team owners and players unions millions of dollars in lost revenue. It would also cost the players valuable playing time. It would cost the fans a lost summer of baseball, the summer that then Yale University president and later baseball commissioner Bart Giammatti wrote "would never be here again."

And it would cost the Cincinnati Reds the National League West.

As the strike neared its end, the lords of baseball cooked up a ridiculous scheme to choose division winners. In each division the team that was in first before the strike would play the team that was in first at the end of the season—a system full of holes, but the people in the commissioner's office thought it would work. The result was a travesty. The Reds wound up being the strongest team in all of baseball that year, but when the strike started they were one-half game behind the Dodgers, so the Dodgers went to the play-offs. At the end of the season, the Reds were one and a half games behind the Astros, so the Astros went to the play-offs.

THE HIT. This single to left center by Pete Rose broke Ty Cobb's record of 4,191 career hits. His son hugged him when he reached first base and the roar of the capacity crowd rattled the stadium. All records are made to be broken? Well, whoever breaks this one will have to play twenty-three years, average 182 hits per season, play an average of 140 games a year, almost never be hurt, play into his forties and, if all that isn't hard enough, be mighty lucky.

125

Yep! It's one of those crazy big Reds umbrellas.

The Reds, whose record (sixty-six wins, forty-two losses) was the best in the majors, went home. Fans were outraged and so were the players. "Everybody on that team felt we were shortchanged," said Tom Seaver, in one of his rare angry moments. "We played hard, every one of us, and we deserved a chance in the play-offs. What happened to us was wrong and it was a disgrace. Baseball should be ashamed of itself."

How good were the Reds in 1981, the year they didn't get an opportunity to win everything? Seaver had an incredible 14-2 record, Mario Soto was 12-9, Bob Berenyi was 9-6. Griffey, Bench, and Concepcion all hit over .300. Foster had twenty-two homers and ninety RBIs in the shortened 108-game season.

Fans with memories in the Queen City immediately recalled the 1919 season and saw parallels. In 1919, the Reds won the pennant and won the World Series over the Chicago White Sox but had the world championship tarnished forever when it was charged the following year that eight players on the White Sox took money to throw the series. Now, in 1981, the team was getting another raw deal, having a possible championship snatched away by some crazy scheme hatched in the commissioner's office in New York.

"We got shafted in 1919, and we got shafted in 1981. It's that simple," said long-time fan Willie DeLuca.

The debacle completely unhinged the Reds. During the following winter, the front office traded away Ken Griffey, Ray

One of many souvenir balls sold at stands outside Riverfront.

126

A fan had some fun with this license plate. The "PR" is for Pete Rose, the "4192" is for Rose's record, and "Marge's Chevrolet" refers to Schott's car company.

Marge Schott, one of the few women owners in the game's history, has always been a lightning rod for news, good and bad. It was Schott who brought Pete Rose back so he could break Ty Cobb's hit record at home. It was Schott who, on instinct, hired Lou Piniella as manager and soon had a world championship.

Knight, and George Foster. Seaver spent much of 1982 injured or sick and went 5-13, his worst year. McNamara was fired in midseason. The Reds slid into last place, losing a record 101 games, and were last again in 1983. The fall from grace was complete.

It was a woman, one of the few in all baseball, who stepped in to salvage what was left of the once proud Big Red Machine. Businesswoman Marge Schott, a colorful and, later, controversial, Cincinnati personality who brought her dogs to the ballpark, bought the team in 1984, and looked to the past to build the team's future. The first thing she did was bring back Pete Rose, and later Tony Perez, to the roaring approval of the fans. Rose was determined to break one of baseball's greatest records, Ty Cobb's total hits, and was closing in. At Montreal, where he was

playing in 1984, he came to within one hundred. Schott wanted him to make history at home where he belonged. Late in 1984 Schott, in one of her finest moments, welcomed Rose back to Cincinnati and named him player-manager.

Feelings about Schott would soon become mixed in Cincinnati. At first players and fans loved her dog, Schotzie, and his successor, Schotzie II, and the way Schott let them have run of the ballpark (where they had their own space in her office). Later, it became tiring. The grounds crew didn't appreciate cleaning up after the animals, fans grew weary of them and the endless awards ceremonies Schott

127

PETE ROSE

Four thousand, two hundred and fifty-six. Even spelled out, it's a lot. That's how many hits—singles, doubles, triples, and home runs—that Pete Rose hit before he finally left baseball. He was the all-time hit leader and also the all-time leader in singles, at bats, and games played. He is second in doubles, fourth in runs scored, and stroked two hundred hits ten years in a row. He is the only player to play five hundred games at five different positions. He was National League MVP in 1973 and World Series MVP in 1975.

Pete Rose was born and raised in Cincinnati and all he ever wanted to do as a kid was play baseball for the Cincinnati Reds. His dream came true. He was one of the anchors of the Big Red Machine and a major reason for its success.

Rose left Cincinnati for Philadelphia in 1980, and in 1983 went to the Montreal Expos. There, at age forty-three, he slapped hit number four thousand. In 1984, owner Marge Schott brought Rose back to Cincinnati as player-manager so he could break the

Pete Chocolate Flavored Beverage 9½ FL. OZ. SHAKE WELL!

There were Rose soda cans . . .

Pete Rose's RESTAURANT PHONE 574-5000

. . . and Rose matchbooks . . .

PETE ROSE 4192 HITS · SEPT. 11, 85

PETE ROSE 4192 HITS · SEPT. 11, 85

. . . and penknives . . .

PETE ROSE WAY E

This is the original street sign that hangs outside Riverfront. Despite the furor over Rose's prison term, the city insisted the street carry his name.

Rose appeared on Pepsi's cards and a commemorative ashtray.

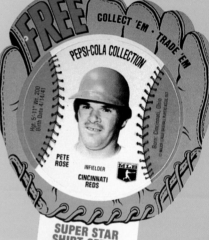

record at home. Rose finally broke it on September 11, 1985, and took a step into immortality.

"It wasn't luck. It wasn't a fluke. It was something I wanted for twenty years, went after, and got," said Rose. "I had a goal and I went after it."

Of course, the flowers wilted for Rose in 1989, when he was suspended from baseball for allegedly betting on games. He later went to jail for failing to pay all of his taxes. He was ruled ineligible to participate in baseball for the rest of his life (or be in the Hall of Fame). He can apply for reinstatement, though, and fans swear that if the doors of Cooperstown ever open for Rose, he will slide into the Hall of Fame face first.

. . . and even scotch.

"Batting Practice" was a 1970s game kids used to improve their swings.

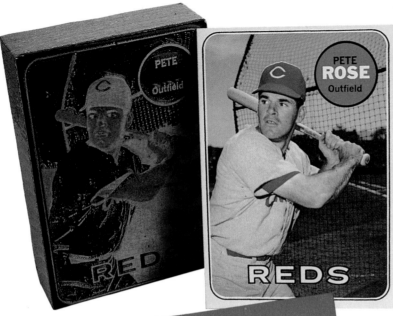

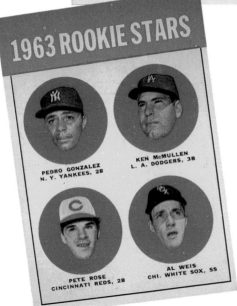

One collector some-
how got a 1970
Topps Pete Rose
card and its original
printing plate.

Pete Rose's rookie
Topps baseball card
is one of the most
valuable around
(those of the other
three guys are not).

conducted on the field before games.
Players complained of the time she called a
team meeting to show pictures of
Schotzie's grave site. She promised Tony
Perez a car when he retired, as she had
Rose, and fans were irate that Perez got a
much cheaper car.

A real storm erupted in the fall of
1992, when an office worker listening in
on a conference call said she heard Schott
make a number of derogatory racial
remarks about black players on her team.
When her remarks hit the airwaves and
newspapers, people across the country
condemned her and demanded some kind
of punishment. Schott made a public apol-
ogy, and major league baseball slapped her
with a year-long suspension, keeping her
out of the game for all of 1993.

On September 11, 1985, Rose broke
Cobb's record with a single to center. As
manager, he did something nearly as
remarkable that year. He took the Reds,
who finished fifth in 1984, to second place,
just five and a half games behind the
Dodgers. Rookie Tom Browning won
twenty games for the club, the first rookie
to win twenty games in thirty-one years.
Reliever John Franco had a 12-3 record. In
the lineup, Dave Parker had perhaps his
best season, hitting .312, with 125 RBIs (he
was second in the MVP voting). Tony
Perez, then forty-three, hit .328. It was the

One ingenious fan talked a printer at the *Cincinnati Post* into giving him the original front-page plate of "The Hit."

This is the bat and ball Rose used to stroke hit number 4,192, breaking Ty Cobb's all-time hit record. Both are signed by Pete.

Even Pete Rose watches were produced in the post-Hit mania.

Cincinnati hosted the All-Star Game the year Riverfront opened, 1970, and again in 1988.

beginning of the "new Reds," an era that would see the team finish second in four consecutive years, the departure of Rose amid a scandal in 1989, and then a world championship in 1990.

Eric Davis arrived in 1986 and hit twenty-seven home runs with a .277 average in the first of several productive seasons with the team. Tagged the next Willie Mays, Davis, using a phenomenally quick batting stroke, socked thirty-seven homers and 100 RBIs in 1987, twenty-six homers and 23 RBIs in 1988, and thirty-four homers and 101 RBIs in 1989. His brilliant career was constantly hampered by injuries, though, and he played rarely in 1989 and 1990; eventually the Reds traded Davis to Los Angeles.

Pete Rose graced just about every baseball magazine cover, even the sticker books, at the start of the 1986 season.

Pete Rose's own very treasured memorabilia. Among the items: his 1973 MVP award, balls from his first and tenth two-hundred-hit seasons, World Series rings, and his 1975 World Series trophy.

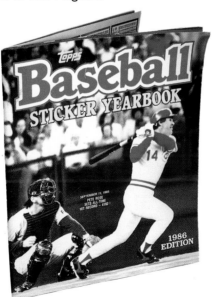

Barry Larkin, who came up in 1986, has become a mainstay in Cincinnati and, with his near .300 batting average, has moved up to icon status in the city, along with members of the 1970s Big Red Machine, and Kluszewski, Post, Robinson, and the stars of the 1930s. What endears him to fans is that he's from Cincinnati, a graduate of Moeller High. His brothers, Mike and Byron, were stars at Moeller, too, and Byron went on to star in basket-

Barry Larkin is the best shortstop in baseball and he is always good. He fights his way out of slumps, helps his teammates, and never gives up.

—CHRIS DELANEY, 14, DAYTON, KENTUCKY

Taking off on runway two is Barry Larkin. Here, on July 10, 1988, Larkin leaps over Phillies' Mike Young to throw to first to complete a double play.

cular, six-foot, 190-pound frame, has been a consistent star for the Reds offensively and defensively. He has had some wonderful seasons. From 1990 to 1992 he hit over .300 and in 1989 had one of the great seasons in Reds history, hitting .342 for half a year before he was injured.

After four second-place finishes, everything unraveled in Cincinnati in 1989 as reports escalated all summer that Pete Rose had bet on baseball games as manager and was under investigation on income tax charges. Finally, in August, Baseball Commissioner Bart Giammatti suspended Rose for life on charges that he had bet on baseball games (though not against his own team). The Reds, in turmoil all year because of the investigations, plunged into fifth place.

Lou Piniella arrived in 1990 to pick up the emotionally tattered Reds, bringing Yankee shortstop Hal Morris with him (Lou, a popular player on the Yankee team that was steamrolled by the Reds in the 1976 series, managed the Yankees in the late 1980s). No one expected much from Cincinnati in 1990 with the team still in turmoil over the Rose situation, Eric Davis still injured, and the pitching staff still ineffective. But, under a new manager who had no connections at all to Cincinnati's past or personnel, the Reds exploded. They won their opening game and stayed

ball at Xavier University in town. "I grew up here when the Big Red Machine was enjoying all those championships, and playing here is all I ever wanted to do," said Larkin. "For me, being a Red is a little boy's dream come true." The mild-mannered Larkin, who has no flab on his mus-

Manager Lou Piniella goes eyeball to eyeball with yet another umpire. Piniella surprised all of Ohio by winning a pennant in his first season, 1990, but left in 1993 after disputes with the front office.

Buttons of 1990 heroes Barry Larkin and Paul O'Neill lean casually against a replica 1950s Reds cap.

in first place all season, wire to wire, the first team to do that since 1969. They won the pennant by five games, but held a ten-game lead most of the way.

The injured Davis still managed to hit twenty-four home runs and collect eighty-four RBIs. Hal Morris hit .340 in 107 games, Mariano Duncan hit .306, and Larkin .301. A diamond in the rough was Chris Sabo, who arrived in 1989 with a 1950s summer-at-the-beach crewcut and wore goggles. The fans liked his appearance, but what they loved about Sabo was his hustle. Not since Pete Rose in his heyday had anyone hustled like Sabo, aggressively running out every ground ball and sliding face first into bases. Sabo was Rookie of the Year in 1989. In 1990, he hit twenty-five homers.

The Reds hitters of 1990 were not at all like the Big Red Machine of the 1970s. The players on the 1990 team were what fans in the 1930s called a "fast team"—they relied on hit-and-run plays, steals, lots of singles, and strategy in the dugout. Except for Larkin, there was no potential Hall of Famer in the 1990 team, but everybody played their best. The Big Red Machine hitters, in contrast, were simply overpowering, wizards of the long ball.

The pitching staff of the 1990 squad, however, was very much like the Big Red Machine staff, and Piniella used them just

REDS FANS

You ask anybody why they love the Reds and they'll tell you it was passed down to them by their fathers, and it was passed to him by his grandfather. And so on, back into time. The great tradition here, being the first pro team back in 1869, means a lot to people and they pass the love of the ball club down over generations. You are born a Reds fan.

—DOROTHY SAVAITCH, 55, OF CINCINNATI

I watch every game on television. If I can't, or I'm working during a day game, I videotape every game and watch it later. Somehow, I see every single game on TV. If the game is not on TV I just listen to the radio.

—MICHELLE BLANEY, 23, OF LOGAN, WEST VIRGINIA

We drive two hours to get here and we come six or seven games a year. Two hours isn't anything to see the Reds. I'd drive twice that.

—CHERYL TUCKER, 36, OF INDIANAPOLIS

A chair from Crosley Field anchors this group of books, banners, and bats of the Big Red Machine years.

We live here and so this is our ball club. Everybody sees the Reds as their team. You go to places like New York or New Orleans and see people walking around with hats from twelve different teams. In Cincinnati people wear just one hat, and it's bright red.

—RICHARD MILLER, OF COVINGTON, KENTUCKY

A local gas station gave away these drinking cups with famous Reds photos on them with a full tank in the 1980s.

All the new arrivals in town become Reds fans. That doesn't happen anywhere else. If a Dodger or Cubs fan moves to St. Louis, he or she isn't going to become a Cards fan. But when people move to Cincinnati they immediately become Reds fans. They get caught up in the excitement of the Reds. They just can't help it.

—EVAN ANDREWS,
MANAGER OF THE BOATHOUSE RESTAURANT,
FILLED TO THE BRIM WITH REDS MEMORABILIA

Who'd have thunk it? The 1990 Reds, picked by most writers to finish near the bottom of the league in April, not only won the division and pennant, but swept the mighty Oakland A's to take the World Series. Players here celebrate on the field in Oakland.

as adroitly as Sparky Anderson had. In the monster seasons of 1975 and 1976, no Reds pitcher won more than fifteen games, but each season six pitchers topped ten games. In 1990, with Piniella looking for the same results, Browning went 15-9, José Rijo 14-8, and Jack Armstrong 12-9. Like Anderson, Piniella used his bullpen frequently and with results. His relievers—Randy Myers, Norm Charlton, and Rob Dibble—were quickly nicknamed the "Nasty Boys" for the way they stared down and shut down hitters when they came into the game. Myers had thirty-one saves that summer, and Dibble had eleven, with an 8-3 record and 1.75 ERA. With a 100-mph fastball, Dibble fanned 136 batters in just ninety-eight innings, striking out more batters than any other NL reliever. He went on to have a phenomenal postseason. Charlton, used as the set-up reliever in middle innings for the first half of the season, was made a starter in July and turned in a 12-9 record. (Comparatively, the Big Red Machine had only one consistent reliever, Rawly Eastwick, who had forty-eight saves in three and a half seasons in the mid-1970s.)

Chris Sabo, here just missing Carney Lansford in the 1990 Series, came to the Reds in 1988 as an unheralded first-year man to replace the injured Buddy Bell. He promptly hit .312 for the first half of the season and went on to win Rookie of the Year honors. Fans loved his goggles and his hustle.

Piniella used the Nasty Boys often in the play-offs against the favored Pirates. The Reds won it in six, clinching the series with Glenn Braggs's sensational over-the-wall catch of a Carmelo Martinez drive in the last inning of game six. The team went into the World Series a heavy underdog against baseball's glamour team, the world champion Oakland A's, who had swept a good Giants team in the 1989 series and beaten up on the American League all through 1990, winning their third straight pennant. They seemed impregnable, having

swept the Red Sox four straight in the American League play-off series.

The A's had everything. On the mound they had the best pitcher in baseball that year, Bob Welch, who won twenty-seven games, and the best pitcher in baseball over the previous few years, Dave Stewart, who had won twenty in a row for four straight seasons and, in 1990, was better than ever. As good as the Reds bullpen was, the A's bullpen was led by Dennis Eckersley, the best closer in baseball, maybe in all of baseball history. In the lineup, Oakland opened the game with Rickey Henderson, a fine hitter and world-record base stealer. They also threw hard-hitting Carney Lansford at their opponents. You want power? The A's had the world-famous "Bash Brothers," José Canseco and Mark McGwire, the strongest home run hitting duo since Mickey Mantle and Roger Maris thirty years before. The A's, in short, had everything (including a manager, Tony LaRussa, who was a lawyer).

Apparently, nobody told the Reds players all of this. They went at the A's like they were a Little League team. Cincinnati battered Oakland in the very first game, 7-0, with Davis hitting a first-inning home run to wake up Dave Stewart. José Rijo pitched a classic game. Game two was close, but the Reds won it 5-4 on a Joe

139

1990 WORLD SERIES

I knew in the second or third inning of the second game that I was never sharper in my life. I have never pitched that well before or that well since. That ball went exactly where I wanted it to go.

—PITCHER JOSÉ RIJO,
WINNER OF GAMES ONE AND FOUR

The first pitch of the 1990 Series, thrown here by José Rijo, was a strike, setting the stage for a phenomenal series by Rijo and the first world championship for Cincinnati in fourteen years.

One word said it all when the Reds took the 1990 world championship, riding the unbelievable arm of José Rijo.

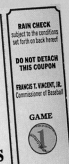

"We felt absolutely no pressure in game one. Everybody expected us to be watching it on TV," said Barry Larkin. Reds stunned baseball and swept the mighty Oakland A's in the 1990 World Series.

The Reds made it to their ninth World Series in 1990, when Lou Piniella led a team of little preseason distinction to a world title.

It's not the final pas de deux to "Swan Lake," but Joe Oliver rounding first and Tony Perez cheering him on as Oliver's hit won game two of the 1990 Series.

We went into that series completely relaxed. Why not? We had nothing to lose. We weren't supposed to win the division or the pennant and we certainly weren't supposed to win the World Series. And how could we, up against the great Oakland A's? We had absolutely nothing to lose, and that's why we won.

—SHORTSTOP BARRY LARKIN

A kid's glove from the 1950s holds two team balls from the 1990 World Series.

said Rijo, sounding eerily similar to Johnny Vander Meer describing his back-to-back no-hitters in 1938. "Sometimes I'd let it go off my fingers and knew it was too high, or too low, but it wound up right where I aimed it anyway. . . . Everything went right for me. I don't think if I pitched twenty more years I could pitch as well as I did in those two games."

Many of the Reds felt they played so well and won so handily because they were underdogs and little was expected of them. "We should not have won the pennant, so all summer there was no pres-

The old and the new. The two bats on the left are Pete Rose models signed by him and others. The two on the right are a José Rijo model and team bat.

A bucketful of baseballs marked "Pitchers" and some equipment sits in the Reds dugout at Riverfront a few minutes before batting practice on a hot August afternoon.

Oliver double that drove in the winning run in the tenth. Oliver hit it off the invincible Eckersley. Billy Hatcher, who had three straight hits in game one, had four more consecutive hits in game two, setting a series record. Game three moved to Oakland, but that didn't help the A's. The Reds bombarded the A's mound staff for seven runs in the third inning and, with the Nasty Boys stepping in late to relieve Browning, won, 8-3. The final game was tight, but the Reds sweated it out and won, 2-1, on a brilliant two-hitter by Rijo.

Rijo seemed in a trance throughout the series. "I never pitched that well in my entire life. The ball went exactly, and I mean exactly, where I wanted it to go,"

142

A boat drifts down the Ohio past Riverfront Stadium.

sure," said Barry Larkin. "No one thought we'd win the play-offs, not at all. Everybody thought we'd lose the series, especially since it was against the awesome Oakland A's. If we lost the series in four straight everyone would have thought we did what we were supposed to do. When you play with no pressure it's a lot easier to do what you want to do. There's no worry; no mental, no emotional factor."

So yet another world championship banner was hoisted over a Reds ballpark, high on top of Riverfront Stadium, overlooking the rolling waters of the Ohio. You can see it fly in the breeze from downtown Cincinnati and from the streets of Covington. And if you stand at the corner of Western Avenue and Findlay, among the old ghosts of Crosley Field and the Palace of the Fans, you can see it best of all.

143

REDS GREATS

JOHNNY BENCH
CATCHER

JOHNNY BENCH

A fiction writer would have had to invent him if the superstar catcher from Oklahoma City had never been born. He started his career with the Reds in August 1967 and was so impressive that the following spring none other than Ted Williams told him right to his face that he'd wind up in the Hall of Fame. He did, of course, on the strength of 389 home runs, 1,376 RBIs, .267 batting average and superb defensive skills over seventeen years.

Bench, who has enormous hands and a stocky, muscular body, was hard working and durable, catching over one hundred games in each of his first thirteen seasons. He was also a World series star for the Reds, hitting .533 in the 1976 series with two homers and averaging .297 over his four series. Bench, also a superb golfer, hit .370 in his thirteen All-Star appearances. He was elected to the Hall of Fame in 1989.

TED KLUSZEWSKI

Kluszewski and his massive arms arrived in Cincinnati in 1947. In his first two full seasons, 1948 and 1949, he hit a total of only twenty home runs, but he exploded for twenty-five in 1950 and then, in a stretch from 1953 to 1956, hit an average of forty-three per season. Perhaps because of his enormous, 225-pound bulk, he was always thought of purely as a fence-buster, but he also hit for average. Over fifteen years, almost all of them with the Reds, Big Klu hit .298. He also led all major leaguers in fielding at first base five times.

Although injuries cut his career short, Klu came back to hit three home runs and drive in ten in the 1959 World Series for the White Sox.

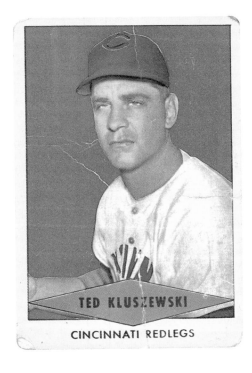

TED KLUSZEWSKI
CINCINNATI REDLEGS

After Reds General Manager Bill DeWitt, in an incredible mistake, traded Robinson away after the 1965 season, Robinson proceeded to win baseball's triple crown, hitting .316, with forty-nine homers and 122 RBIs, becoming the only man ever to be named MVP in both leagues. He went on to become the first black manager in baseball, for Cleveland in 1975. Robinson was enshrined in Cooperstown in 1982.

PETE ROSE

PETE ROSE

A jail term for income-tax evasion and expulsion from baseball, which made him the Shoeless Joe Jackson of his era, overshadowed Rose's truly monumental accomplishments. Over twenty-four years, he set records with 4,256 hits, 3,215 singles, 14,053 at bats, and 3,562 games played. He tied the National League's venerable consecutive-game hitting streak—forty-four games—set back in the nineteenth century by Wee Willie Keeler. He had more than two hundred hits in a season ten times, and over one hundred hits in twenty-three seasons. He did all of this by challenging pitchers with a stance that crowded the plate. An aggressive runner and player who stole hundreds of bases face first, Rose earned his nickname "Charlie Hustle" in spring training of his rookie year when a veteran said that Rose ran out routine groundouts like it was the last game of the World Series.

Rose was not only in remarkable physical shape, but mentally steeled himself for a long career in baseball regardless of events. When, after miserable seasons in Montreal in 1983 and 1984 it appeared that Rose was washed up, and that Ty Cobb's all-time hit record would stand forever, he was brought back to Cincinnati for one last hurrah as player-manager and responded with a .365 batting average and 107 hits that season. In three years at the helm, Rose took the Reds to respectable second place finishes each season.

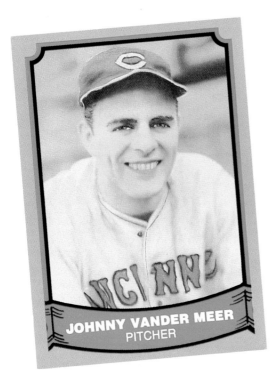

JOHNNY VANDER MEER
PITCHER

HARRY WRIGHT

A transplanted English cricket star, Wright was fascinated by the possibilities of early baseball in America. He became one of the fathers of the game, playing in the first official contest in 1845 and later becoming a force on the Knickerbockers, New York's premier team. Wright, who sported a moustache and rather scraggly beard, was hired by a Cincinnati men's club to form the first all-professional team. In 1869 he and took the team on a national tour that firmly entrenched baseball as a spectator sport.

That was the start of a long career as manager. Wright moved to the Boston Red Stockings in 1871 as skipper and piloted them to two National Association pennants. Wright and Albert Spalding took the team on a tour of England in 1874. Wright later became manager of the Boston Red Caps in the early years of the National League (1876 to 1894), winning two titles with them. An experimenter, Wright introduced the practice of one fielder backing up another. His brother, George, a fine hitter, played on all of his teams. Harry Wright was inducted into the Hall of Fame in 1953.

JOHNNY VANDER MEER

The "Dutch Master" won a niche in American sports history when he hurled back-to-back no-hitters in 1938 (and then went seven hitless innings a few days later). That feat was the highlight of a long and impressive career. Vander Meer was the minor league player of the year in 1936, just before he moved up to the Reds, whom he impressed quickly, winning fifteen games in 1938. In four seasons from 1941 to 1946, the personable Vander Meer, a sturdy six-footer who had a quick smile for everyone, won fifty-nine games and in 1943 he tied Carl Hubbell's record by fanning six batters in the All-Star Game. Two years of naval duty in World War II and later arm trouble cut short his career.

REDS STATS

REDS ALL-TIME PITCHING LEADERS (SINCE 1900)

WON LOST
Bill Thomas.....................383–346
Joe Martina.....................349–277
George Payne..................348–262
Tony Freitas....................342–238
Alex McColl....................332–263
Ken Penner.....................330–284
Lefty George...................327–285
Dick Barrett....................325–257
Spider Baum...................325–280
Ramon Arano.................324–247
Earl Caldwell..................321–277
Willard Mains.................318–179
Paul Wachtel..................317–221
Frank Shellenback..........315–192
Clyde Barfoot.................314–243
Jack Brillheart................308–264
Sam Gibson...................307–200
Bill Hughes....................302–248
Harry Smythe.................301–221
Harry Krause..................300–249

STRIKEOUTS
George Brunet.................3,175
Joe Martina....................2,770
Jackie Reid.....................2,694
Hooks Iott.....................2,561
Dick Barrett...................2,512
Jodie Phipps..................2,447
Woody Rich...................2,405
Bill Bailey......................2,375
Aurelio Monteagudo.........2,361
Paul Fittery....................2,359

GAMES
Bill Thomas.....................1,015
Jim Brillheart....................956
George Payne...................900
Ken Penner......................869
Alex McColl.....................865
Earl Caldwell....................859
Walter Tauscher................856
Bobby Tiefenaue...............849
Joe Martin.......................833
Karl Black........................814

20-WIN SEASONS
Spider Baum...........................9
Tony Freitas............................9
Dick Barrett.............................8
Joe Pate..................................7
Joe Martina.............................7
Charles (Sea Lion) Hall.............7
George Boehler........................7
Herschel Prough......................7
Willard Mains..........................7
Doc Crandall...........................6
Sam Gibson.............................6
John Ogden..............................6
Paul Wachtel............................6
James Middleton.......................6

LIFETIME PITCHING PERCENTAGE LEADERS

PITCHER	DATES	WON–LOST	PCT.
John Ogden	1918–1934	213–103	.674
Joe Pate	1911–1932	257–134	.657
Willard Mains	1887–1906	318–179	.640
Chet Covington	1939–1953	220–126	.636
Bobby Tiefenauer	1948–1969	162–96	.628
Stoney McGlynn	1902–1915	182–109	.625
Frank Shellenback	1917–1938	315–192	.621
Rube Parnham	1914–1927	167–102	.621
Rube Vickers	1902–1914	217–134	.618
Jodie Phipps	1939–1957	275–172	.615
Jimmy H. Walkup	1915–1934	259–164	.612
Tom Sheehan	1913–1934	260–166	.610
Sam Gibson	1923–1949	307–200	.606
Doc Crandall	1906–1929	249–163	.604
Jimmy Zinn	1915–1939	295–198	.598
Cliff Markle	1913–1928	211–144	.594

149

REDS ALL-TIME BATTING LEADERS

HITS

Spencer Harris	3,617
Harry Strohm	3,486
Eddie Hock	3,474
George Whiteman	3,388
Fred Henry	3,384
Jigger Statz	3,356
Ray French	3,254
Chet Chadbourne	3,216
Hugh Luby	3,169
Ray O'Brien	3,152
Jay Kirke	3,165
Jim Poole	3,150
John Gill	3,141
Bernard Uhalt	3,120
Vinicio Garcia	3,116
Buster Chatham	3,067
Larry Barton	3,045
Smead Jolley	3,037
Mel Simons	3,031

HOME RUNS

Hector Espino	484
Buzz Arlett	432
Nick Cullop	420
Merv Commors	400
Joe Hauser	399
Bobby Prescott	398
Jack Graham	384
Ted Gullic	370
Gordon Nell	365
Leo "Muscle" Shoals	362
Jack Pierce	395

RBIS

Nick Cullop	1,857
Buzz Arlett	1,786
Jim Poole	1,785
Spencer Harris	1,769
Larry Barton	1,751
Johnny Gill	1,743
George Ferrell	1,716
Hector Espino	1,678
Smead Jolley	1,631
Merv Connors	1,629

RUNS

Spencer Harris	2,287
George Hogriever	2,046
Eddie Hock	2,007
Jigger Statz	1,996
George Whiteman	1,885
Kid Mohler	1,811
Frenchy Uhalt	1,786
Bunny Brief	1,776
Ray French	1,769
Buster Chatham	1,739

DOUBLES

Spencer Harris	743
Fred Henry	675
George Whiteman	673
Johnny Gill	667
Jim Poole	662
Harry Strohm	658
Ray O'Brien	642
Larry Barton	634
Smead Jolley	612
Lyman Lamb	608

TRIPLES

Joe Riggert	228
Fred Henry	200
George Whiteman	196
Fred Nicholson	195
Lee Riley	195
Jim Murray	191
Ray O'Brien	186
Stanley Keyes	185
Ray Powell	183
Buster Chatham	182

STOLEN BASES

George Hogreiver	948
Kid Mohler	776
Count Campau	682
Alex Reilley	676
Bill Lane	670
John Duffy	626
Merlin Kopp	604
Dave Mann	601
Carlos Bernier	594
Tony Thebo	593

AVERAGE

Ike Boone	.370
Ox Eckhardt	.367
Smead Jolley	.366
Don Stokes	.365
Carl East	.364
Bill Bagwell	.360
Bill George	.358
Dan Boone	.356
Jack Bentley	.354
Al Pinkston	.352
Claude Salano	.360
Tom Pyle	.354
Dean Stafford	.351
Bill Wright	.351
Pete Hughes	.350

BATTING TITLES

Smead Jolley	6
Ike Boone	5
Moose Clabaugh	5
Ox Eckhardt	5
Frank Huelsman	5
Sheldon Lejeune	5
Hector Espino	5
Al Pinkston	5

HOME RUN TITLES

Ken Guettler	8
Bunny Brief	7
Ray Perry	7
Leo Shoals	7
Norman Small	7
Mervyn Connors	6
Ted Norbert	6

200-HIT SEASONS

Jigger Statz	11
Buzz Arlett	7
Bunny Brief	7
Chester Chadbourne	7
Smead Jolley	7
Don Stokes	7
Edward Mulligan	6

100-RBI SEASONS

Buzz Arlett	12
Mervyn Connors	11
Smead Jolley	9
Pete Hughes	9
Dean Stafford	9
Bunny Brief	8
Gordon Nell	8
Ray Perry	8
Ollie Tucker	8
Ab Wright	8
Isaac Palmer	8

20-HOMERS SEASONS

Mervyn Connors	12
Nick Cullop	12
Hector Espino	12
Jack Graham	12
Buzz Arlett	11
Joe Hauser	10

30-HOMERS SEASONS

Buzz Arlett	8
Joe Bauman	6
Jack Graham	6
Joe Hauser	6
Gordon Nell	6
Norman Small	6

40-HOMERS SEASONS

Joe Bauman	5
Gordon Nell	5

50-HOMERS SEASONS

Joe Bauman	3
Joe Hauser	2
Bob Crues	2
Pud Miller	2
Grank Gravino	2
Steve Bilko	2

REDS .300 HITTERS (1900–1991) (MIN. 400 AT-BATS)

RANK	PLAYER	PCT.	YEAR
1	C. Seymour	.377	1905
2	B. Hargrave	.353	1926
3	E. Roush	.352	1921
4	E. Roush	.351	1923
	M. Donlin	.351	1903
6	E. Roush	.348	1924
	P. Rose	.348	1969
8	V. Pinson	.343	1961
9	C. Seymour	.342	1903
	E. Lombardi	.342	1938
	F. Robinson	.342	1962
12	J. Beckley	.341	1900
	E. Roush	.341	1917
14	G. Harper	.340	1922
15	H. Chase	.339	1916
	E, Roush	.339	1920
	E. Roush	.339	1925
18	P. Rose	.338	1973
19	J. Daubert	.336	1922
	K. Griffey	.336	1976
21	P. Rose	.335	1968
22	S. Crawford	.333	1902
	E. Roush	.333	1918
	H. Hellmann	.333	1930
25	F. McCormick	.332	1939
26	S. Crawford	.330	1901
	J. Beckley	.330	1902
28	P. Duncan	.328	1922
29	J. Beckley	.327	1903
	P. Duncan	.327	1923
	F. McCormick	.327	1938
	J. Morgan	.327	1975
33	B. Herman	.326	1932
	K. Cuyler	.326	1936
	T. Kluszewski	.326	1954
36	S. Barry	.324	1905
	J. Stripp	.324	1931
38	E. Roush	.323	1926
	I. Goodman	.323	1939
	F. Robinson	.323	1961
	P. Rose	.323	1976
42	H. Critz	.322	1924
	F. Robinson	.322	1957
44	E. Roush	.321	1919
45	H. Groh	.320	1918
	T. Kluszewski	.320	1952
	J. Morgan	.320	1976
	G. Foster	.320	1977
49	C. Walker	.318	1925
	K. Griffey	.318	1977
	R. Knight	.318	1979
	H. Morris	.318	1991
53	A. Marsans	.317	1912
	T. Perez	.317	1970
	P. Rose	.317	1975
56	J. Barrett	.316	1900
	T. Kluszewski	.316	1953
	V. Pinson	.316	1959
	P. Rose	.316	1970
	B. Tolan	.316	1970
61	H. Hendrick	.315	1931
	T. Cuccinello	.315	1931
	A. Johnson	.315	1969
64	T. Kluszewski	.314	1955
	T. Perez	.314	1973
66	C. Seymour	.313	1904
	C. Walker	.313	1929
	L. Scarsella	.313	1936
	V. Pinson	.313	1963
	P. Rose	.313	1966
71	H. Steinfeldt	.312	1903
	T. Cuccinello	.312	1930
	J. Lynch	.312	1958
	P. Rose	.312	1965
	A. Johnson	.312	1968
	D. Parker	.312	1985
77	J. Wyrostek	.311	1951
	F. Robinson	.311	1959
	J. Temple	.311	1959
	P. Rose	.311	1977
	K. Griffey	.311	1981
82	M. Mitchell	.310	1909
	H. Groh	.310	1919
84	F. McCormick	.309	1940
	T. Kluszewski	.309	1949
	W. Post	.309	1959
87	D. Hoblitzell	.308	1909
	P. Duncan	.308	1921
	G. Bell	.308	1955
90	J. Beckley	.307	1901
	T. Griffith	.307	1915
	C. Walker	.307	1930
	W. Berger	.307	1938
	T. Kluszewski	.307	1950
	J. Temple	.307	1954
	P. Rose	.307	1972
	C. Geronimo	.307	1976
98	J. Daubert	.306	1921
	B. Pinelli	.306	1924
	C. Walker	.306	1926
	J. Stripp	.306	1930
	S. Burgess	.306	1955
	J. Temple	.306	1958
	F. Robinson	.306	1964
	G. Foster	.306	1976
	D. Concepcion	.306	1981
	M. Duncan	.306	1990
108	B. Pinelli	.305	1922
	E. Allen	.305	1928
	E. Lombardi	.305	1934
	F. McCormick	.305	1944
	V. Pinson	.305	1965
	B. Tolan	.305	1969
	K. Griffey	.305	1975
115	H. Groh	.304	1917
	J. Daubert	.304	1920
	P. Rose	.304	1971
118	E. Lombardi	.303	1932
	C. Hafey	.303	1933
	F. McCormick	.303	1943
	D. Collins	.303	1980
122	T. Kluszewski	.302	1956
	P. Rose	.302	1978
	G. Foster	.302	1979
	B. Larkin	.302	1991
126	E. Tipton	.301	1944
	P. Rose	.301	1967
	D. Concepcion	.301	1978
	B. Larkin	.301	1990
	C. Sabo	.301	1991
131	D. Paskert	.300	1910
	M. Swanson	.300	1929
	M. McCormick	.300	1940
	G. Bell	.300	1953
	G. Foster	.300	1975
	D. Driessen	.300	1977

AUTOGRAPH PAGE

BIBLIOGRAPHY

Anderson, Sparky. *The Main Spark.* New York: Doubleday, 1978.

Brosnan, Jim. *Pennant Race.* New York: Harper & Row, 1962.

————. *The Long Season.* Evanston, Ill.: Holtzman Press, 1960.

Hertzel, Bob. *The Big Red Machine.* Englewood Cliffs, N.J.: Prentice-Hall, 1976.

Honig, Donald. *The Cincinnati Reds.* New York: Simon and Schuster, 1990.

Rose, Pete, and Roger Kahn. *Pete Rose: My Story.* New York: Macmillan, 1989.

Seymour, Harold. *Baseball: The Early Years.* New York: Oxford University Press, 1960.

Shatzkin, Mike. *The Ballplayers.* New York: William Morrow, 1990.

Sokolove, Mike. *Hustle: The Myth, Life and Lies of Pete Rose.* New York: Simon and Schuster, 1990.

Wolff, Rick, ed. *The Baseball Encyclopedia.* New York: Macmillan, 1990.

INDEX

154

PHOTOGRAPHY CREDITS

All photography by David M. Spindel, with the following exceptions: AP/Wide World Photos: 68 top left, 100 right, 135 top; Cincinnati Historical Society: 23, 27, 30, 42 bottom, 70 top left; Bob Bartosz, Wenonah, New Jersey: 120 top; National Baseball Library & Archive, Cooperstown, New York: 14, 17 bottom left, 19, 20, 25 right, 39 bottom right, 40, 45 bottom left, 46, 57, 58, 63, 64 both, 65, 78, 83 top right, 88 bottom right, 92 bottom right, 94 top, 95, 105 top left, 113 bottom left; Earl D. Payne/ Copyright © Robert B. Payne, Colorado Springs, CO: 62; Reuters/Bettman: 127 right, 140 bottom left; Rochester Democrat and Chronicle: 85 bottom left, 87 top left; University of Cincinnati, Archives & Rare Books Department: 29 top left, 52 bottom, 53 bottom right, 122; UPI/Bettmann: 60, 68 bottom right, 91 left, 102, 104, 108, 109 left, 124, 134, 138, 139, 141 bottom left.